This is number one hundred and twenty-two
in the second numbered series of the
Miegunyah Volumes
made possible by the
Miegunyah Fund
established by bequests
under the wills of
Sir Russell and Lady Grimwade.

'Miegunyah' was the home of
Mab and Russell Grimwade
from 1911 to 1955.

OCEANS

Recipes and Stories from Australia's Coastline

ANDREW DWYER

with photography by John Hay

THE
MIEGUNYAH
PRESS

THE MIEGUNYAH PRESS
An imprint of Melbourne University Publishing Limited
187 Grattan Street, Carlton, Victoria 3053, Australia
mup-info@unimelb.edu.au
www.mup.com.au

First published 2009
Text © Andrew Dwyer, 2009
Photography © John Hay, 2009 (unless otherwise indicated in picture credits)
Design and typography © Melbourne University Publishing Limited, 2009

Designed by Phil Campbell
Printed in China by Imago

National Library of Australia Cataloguing-in-Publication entry:

Dwyer, Andrew.
Oceans: recipes and stories from Australia's coastline / Andrew Dwyer; photographer John Hay.

9780522856224 (hbk.)

Includes index.
Bibliography.

Cookery (Fish)

Other authors/contributors:
Hay, John, 1949–

641.692

Note: This book uses Australian cups (250 ml or 8 1/2 fl oz) and tablespoons (20 ml or 4 teaspoons).

CONTENTS

INTRODUCTION

Australia is an island continent. Four seas and three major oceans wash her 34 280-kilometre-long coastline. They contain her in almost complete isolation. They have allowed her to develop unique flora and fauna and for thousands of years they have protected her from invasion. Australia's rocks are some of the oldest on the planet, and yet she broke away from Gondwanaland only 45 million years ago, to become the youngest continent on earth. The Southern Ocean poured into the rift created between Australia and Antarctica; two circumpolar currents refrigerate her southern coastlines. To the east, the boundless blue of the Pacific Ocean is unbroken save for a few small atolls and the odd island chain until the tumultuous tectonic shore of the Americas rises to restrain it, some 15 000 kilometres away. To the west, the third-largest and warmest oceanic division on the planet—the Indian Ocean—stretches almost 10 000 kilometres, to the shores of Africa.

Separating Australia from New Zealand is the Tasman Sea, referred to affectionately by Australasians on both sides of its sweep as 'the Ditch', a euphemism that belies the ferocity of the savage storms that blow up from the Antarctic, striking fear into the hearts of trans-Tasman mariners. Further north is the Coral Sea—a maze of islands, cays and reefs—often benign and calm during the winter months, but wild and angry during the monsoon, when cyclones vent their fury upon the northern coastline. Torres Strait separates the Coral Sea from the Arafura Sea, punctuated by a series of reefs and sand banks that crowd the narrow waters between Papua New Guinea and Cape York. Further west is the Timor Sea, also a breeding ground for cyclones that ravage the Kimberley, Pilbara and Gascoyne coasts. It is generally shallow, except at the Timor Trough, where it plunges to an abyssal depth of 3300 metres.

The Australian coastline is diverse in its landforms and breathtakingly beautiful. Like all things Australian, it is unfamiliar and strange to newcomers. It doesn't give up its secrets easily. The first navigators, James Grant, Matthew Flinders, and Nicolas Baudin, failed to discover the mouths of the major rivers, which were obscured to the sea by mud flats, or sand bars and dunes, generally lacking the wide, deep estuaries so familiar to Georgian navigators. Crocodile-infested mangrove swamps and mud flats obfuscate the opaque turquoise waters of the Gulf of Carpentaria, home of the dugong, the turtle and the feisty Spanish mackerel. They cheated the explorers Robert O'Hara Burke and William John Wills from seeing the northern coast during their ill-fated attempt to cross the Australian continent, in 1861.

From the tip of Cape York, the Great Barrier Reef stretches 2600 kilometres southward along the Queensland coast. It is the world's biggest living thing. Now a paradise for aquatic recreation, it was the nemesis of the early navigators, puncturing the hull of James Cook's *Endeavour* and sinking the *Pandora* when she was returning to England with the captured *Bounty* mutineers in irons. The reef continues to demand constant vigilance from ships' masters to navigate a safe passage though its labyrinthine coral.

The East Australian Current flows southward at speeds of up to 7 knots, bringing warm water from the tropics and delivering it into the cold waters of the Tasman Sea, a marine superhighway transporting tropical fish to southern latitudes. At its peak, in February, it moves a staggering 30 million cubic metres of water every second. The Great Dividing Range provides the backdrop to the eastern seaboard, where, on a thin strip of land separating mountains from sea, the majority of Australia's human population is domiciled. The range continually changes shape as one sails south. In the Daintree, the deep-blue rainforest-carpeted hills descend steeply to the tropical coast. North of Brisbane, the peculiar volcanic plugs of the Glasshouse Mountains rise dramatically in perpendicular pillars to heights of 500 metres, and further south on the border of New South Wales is the Mount Warning caldera, each morning the first land on the continent touched by the sun's rays. Sandstone cliffs tower above the sea around the entrance to Sydney Harbour, and southward beyond Cape Jervis the coastline is indented with tranquil bays and beaches, its backdrop the spectacular Southern Highlands. In 1770, one singular sandstone bluff shaped like a woman's nipple attracted the sea-weary eyes of James Cook, who in the circumspect manner befitting a Yorkshireman of his times gave it the unimaginative name Pigeon House Mountain.

At Cape Howe, the coast turns westward into Bass Strait, the waters separating the mainland from Tasmania. No longer under the influence of the east-coast current, the waters drop in temperature, chilled

by the icy Southern Ocean. The sweeping coastline of Croajingolong and the Ninety Mile Beach ends at the spectacular Wilsons Promontory, the southernmost point of mainland Australia, which juts into Bass Strait. Dense eucalypt forests descend to a wilderness coast of granite headlands interspersed with delightful beaches of dazzling white sand and turquoise water.

To the south of Wilson's Promontory is the great rock pyramid of Rodondo Island, thrusting defiantly 350 metres straight out of Bass Strait. Further south is a chain of islands including the Kent, Hogan, Curtis and Furneaux groups. The relatively short distance between each group allows small vessels to island-hop across one of the most treacherous stretches of water in the world, from the mainland to Tasmania.

From the pristine beaches of the Bay of Fires southward, the east coast of Tasmania rises to dizzying heights at the Freycinet Peninsula. The perpendicular walls of the aptly named Remarkables tower above the annular stretch of dazzling white sand at Wineglass Bay, consistently voted one of the most beautiful beaches in the world. Further south, past Maria Island, the ramparts of the Tasman Peninsula form a gateway to Storm Bay and the Derwent River Estuary. On the west side of the bay, Bruny Island protects the D'Entrecasteaux Channel from the Southern Ocean. The wide sweep of Adventure Bay is where James Cook in the *Endeavour* and ten years later William Bligh in the *Bounty* dropped anchor to take on water and timber during their epic journeys to the South Seas.

From South East Cape to Strahan, past Australia's southernmost lighthouse, at the wild and windblown Maatsuyker Island, the only safe anchorage is at remote Port Davey, where rain falls on 250 days of the year. The mountains look down on a deep, sheltered estuary, a drowned river valley where a layer of dark tannin-stained water percolates out of the dense rainforest of the south-western wilderness and overlies the clear marine water beneath, the inversion creating a rare habitat for marine species that would normally live only at far greater depths. The only way to reach it is by boat, by plane, or by foot. There are no roads. The west coast is a wild place where the Southern Ocean, driven by the howling winds of the roaring forties, pounds relentlessly against the shores. Wave heights of 20 metres are not uncommon. The entrance to Strahan is through the notorious Hells Gates, a safe mooring amid the serene tannin-stained waters of Macquarie Harbour.

The north coast of Tasmania is relatively tame, the rustic fishing village of Stanley nestled beneath 'The Nut', the town of Penguin, and Devonport, where the two Spirit of Tasmania ferries arrive and depart daily, providing an umbilical link with the mainland. Their journey north-west across Bass Strait to Melbourne takes them through the well-hidden entrance to Port Phillip Bay, which for fourteen years after Australia was settled eluded European explorers. In 1798 Flinders and Bass missed it, as did Grant in 1801. Its 2-mile-wide entrance, the treacherous Rip, has claimed over fifty vessels. With the Lonsdale Reef to the west and the Nepean Reef to the east, the tide surges through the narrow gap at between 5 and 7 knots, with a deep trough in the centre creating a whirlpool where flow and ebb meet, and the water surges and is tossed into a 'rough up', perfect conditions for catching the magnificent kingfish yellow-tail.

Further west, the slopes of the Otway Ranges fall to the coast. During the Great Depression, workers carved the Great Ocean Road into their cliffs; hewed out of the rock by hand, it is one of the world's great coastal drives. Moonlight Head, the highest headland in Australia, rises over 120 metres above the western gateway to Bass Strait. At its base, a rusty anchor, all that visibly remains of the wreck of the *Fiji*, marks the eastern end of the Shipwreck Coast, where over two hundred ships went to their watery graves. It is a bleak, inhospitable coastline feared by navigators, who gave its limestone features colourful names like the Sow and Piglets (changed to the sanitised Twelve Apostles by the local tourist board in the early twentieth century). Hidden in the limestone cliffs is Loch Ard Gorge, site of one of Australia's worst maritime catastrophes.

Beyond Cape Bridgewater and the sand hills of Discovery Bay, the coast trends north-west, a rugged stretch of limestone cliffs perched on the very edge of the continental shelf. Rounding Cape Jaffa, the waters open into Lacepede Bay, where the swell is choked by vast seagrass fields that are the feeding grounds for schools of the superb King George whiting. The Younghusband Peninsula, an 80-kilometre-long spit of dune that shelters the Coorong from the Southern Ocean, ends at the mouth of the Murray River, which is often shallow enough to wade across, a modest end to Australia's largest river. On these beaches, between the low- and high-water line, one can dig for the magnificent Goolwa cockles. This is the south-eastern edge of Encounter Bay, the site of the famed meeting in 1802 between Flinders and Baudin. The seas narrow into the Backstairs Passage, the strait separating Kangaroo Island from the mainland. South of Kangaroo Island, beneath the Southern Ocean, lie the Murray Canyons. Here the coastal slope is steeper than anywhere else on the Australian continental margin, and drops from 200 metres to an abyssal 5000 metres in depth over just 40 kilometres. Its cliffs tower over 2 kilometres high, rivalling those of Arizona's Grand Canyon.

The coastline rises around the bald headlands of Cape Jervis and heads north to the beaches of Adelaide and the Gulf St Vincent. Beyond is Spencer Gulf, which juts 300 kilometres north into the Outback. At the head of the gulf lie the northernmost mangrove swamps in Southern Australia, teeming with delicious blue swimmer crabs. To the western edge of Spencer Gulf is the Eyre Peninsula, the grain bowl of Australia. At its southern tip is Port Lincoln, the home of Australia's tuna industry. Round Cape Catastrophe the coast extends north-west, punctuated with the inlets of Coffin, Streaky and Denial bays, where farms produce magnificent Pacific oysters in pure, unpolluted waters. Further north-west is a desert coastline, alternating from pure white sand dunes to limestone cliffs and deserted beaches.

Westward from of the head of the Great Australian Bight, the dramatic Bunda Cliffs stretch for hundreds of kilometres. The vast treeless limestone plateau aptly named the Nullarbor Plain drops abruptly 100 metres into the Southern Ocean. There are few places on earth where the terrestrial maritime delineation is so singularly spectacular. As Matthew Flinders sailed beneath these cliffs in January 1802, he remarked that their tops were 'almost as level as the horizon of the sea'.

The cliffs of the bight gradually recede and the Southern Ocean washes the hundred-odd granite islands that form the Archipelago of the Recherche. Devoid of introduced cats and foxes, these islands provide refuge to species of animals now extinct on the mainland, like the stick nest rat and the burrowing bettong. In 1991 the 174-metre-long Japanese bulk carrier *Sanko Harvest* slammed into a reef here and sank, creating the second-largest dive wreck in the world.

West from here is a magnificent coastline of granite massifs, secluded beaches and harbours all the way to the black dolerite cliffs of Cape Howe and on to the lighthouse at Cape Leeuwin, the most south-westerly point on the Australian mainland and the junction of the Southern and Indian oceans. The Leeuwin Current rips past the cape and swings across to South Australia, ending up as the Zeehan Current off the west coast of Tasmania. While not as large as the east-coast current, the Leeuwin Current brings warm water south from the Timor Sea, allowing tropical reefs to prosper as far south as the Houtman Abrolhos Islands, west of Geraldton, site of the gruesome *Batavia* mutiny in 1629.

Further north is Steep Point, the westernmost tip of mainland Australia and the entrance to Shark Bay, named by the buccaneer, explorer and naturalist William Dampier. Here in the warm saline waters there are living stromatolites, domes of cyanobacteria thought by scientists to be the oldest forms of life on earth.

The Ningaloo Reef, Australia's largest fringing coral reef, runs northward to the North West Cape near Exmouth, where the coast swings north-east to the Pilbara Coast. Here the bellies of great ships are filled with iron ore at some of the largest resource ports on earth: Karratha, Dampier and Port Hedland. Beyond the Eighty Mile Beach is the pearling port of Broome, in Roebuck Bay. At Cable Beach tourists from around the world take camel rides and watch the sun set over the Indian Ocean, where the iron-red sand blown in from the adjoining Great Sandy Desert mingles with the pure white sand of the Indian Ocean. The area has a phenomenal 10-metre tidal variation. Beyond Cape Leveque, the rugged rocks, deep bays, wide tidal mud flats and gorges of the Kimberley Coast stretch on for a seeming eternity, until the Northern Territory border is reached.

The oceans define Australia culturally as well as geographically, having a profound influence on our national psyche. Most Australians live by the sea, clinging to a narrow band of coast, preferring to gaze outward to the blue ocean horizon than inland to the vast arid rangeland. The heart of the continent remains largely uninhabited.

Australia's modern history is steeped in a maritime tradition that began in 1787 when the British Admiralty commissioned the First Fleet and sent it to establish Australia as a penal colony. Administered by the navy, the bellies of its ships were stuffed full of prisoners under marine guard. Its naval commander, Captain Arthur Phillip, became the colony's first governor.

At first the immigrants looked longingly eastward to the horizon of the Pacific, from whence came ships bringing supplies, news from home and sometimes even the chance to leave. The oceans formed the fledgling penal colony's impenetrable wall. Escape was unlikely, if not impossible. The journey to Australia was long, arduous and perilous. Those ships that didn't disappear in the wastes of the Southern Ocean often slammed into the Australian coastline just hours from their destination. The coast is peppered with countless shipwrecks, each with its own panoply of tragedies, dramas and human misery.

Just as the oceans protected our island nation from invasion, they also provided a means to attack us. In the 1870s, suspecting an imminent Russian invasion, the entrance to Port Phillip was fortified and became known as the 'Gibraltar of the South'. In both world wars, Fort Nepean claimed the distinction of firing the first British artillery shell in anger. In 1914 a shot was put across the bows of the German vessel *Pfalz*, an outbound merchantman that was subsequently captured, and in 1939 it fired on the *Stassfurt*, a merchantman that narrowly escaped by scurrying seaward. The World War I prime minister Billy Hughes' infamous statement that Australia was a 'tiny white drop in a coloured ocean' reflected not only our Eurocentric sense of loneliness and isolation, but also the fear that expansionist Asia to the north threatened our soft white underbelly. That threat was eventually realised when Japanese bombers flew across the Arafura Sea to Darwin in February 1942, disgorging more bombs than all those dropped during their attack on Pearl Harbor. When the smoke of World War II cleared, migrant ships carried tens of thousands of emigrants escaping war-torn Europe across the oceans to seek a better life in the new world.

The maritime history of Australia presents a machismo that belies another entirely different relationship that Australians have with the sea. From the early days of settlement, we have gone to the sea for recreation. We learnt to embrace the beach, to fish, boat, swim and surf. Our beaches remain today a place to forget the confines of the suburbs, to realise a sense of space and location, and to cleanse our bodies and souls. They are a place where we get sand between our toes, salt water on our skin and, against better judgement, a bronze suntan. My childhood doctor, to treat most minor ailments, prescribed a dip in salt water.

In 1894, only three years after the establishment of the Royal Lifesaving Society in Britain, an Australian branch was formed in New South Wales. Today over a million Australians take a Royal Life Saving course every year. Over six thousand competitors and officials gather each year at a beach for the Annual Surf Lifesaving Championships, where suntanned athletes with bare feet, broad shoulders, rippling muscles and the signature red-and-yellow cotton caps compete in all manner of beach sports that are televised live to a watching nation.

In 1915, Hawaiian Duke Kahanamoku—founding member of a surf club called The Beach Boys of Waikiki—visited Australia and introduced surfing to the Boomerang Camp at Freshwater Beach, near Sydney. Australians took to the sport like ducks to water. From the stunning Gold Coast Beaches at Surfers Paradise to the jagged, shark-infested limestone shelves off Cactus Beach in the Great Australian Bight, the endlessly diverse coastline moulds the rollers that pound against her shores into perfect surfing waves. Every Easter the surfing eyes of the world turn towards Torquay in Western Victoria, where since 1961 the cream of the world's surfing talent has competed to win the Bells Beach Surf Classic. Fashion houses like Rip Curl and Quicksilver generate a fortune exporting Australian surf chic to the world.

Australian's love of boating is evidenced on any sunny day, when flotillas of small craft crowd Sydney Harbour or Melbourne's Port Phillip Bay, the D'Entrecasteaux Channel south of Hobart, Moreton Bay near Brisbane, or any other of the hundreds of harbours and waterways that ring the continent. The nation stops every year to watch the sleek maxi-yachts round the Tasman Peninsula into Storm Bay and sail up the Derwent Estuary to complete one of the world's toughest blue water races, the Sydney to Hobart.

Indigenous Australians have for perhaps 60 000 years developed a deep relationship with the sea. As the Inuit-Eskimos have over sixty names for different types of snow, so Torres Strait Islanders have some eighty words describing different tides. The solid-canoe technology of South-East Asia spread all the way down the east coast, and mother of pearl was traded extensively along the trade routes. At Lake Condah in Western Victoria, elaborate fish traps were built from the local volcanic stone to trap migratory eels in the Darlot Creek. The skills displayed by Aboriginal hunters was not lost on the Europeans. The navigators Matthew Flinders and Philip King highly regarded their guide Bungaree's skill at spearing fish, and there are endless stories of the extraordinary dexterity, speed and accuracy in spearing, trapping and diving for seafood that was displayed by Aboriginal people.

After the arrival of the First Fleet, fish augmented the half-starved immigrants' diet, and small boats hauled fishing nets daily in Sydney Harbour. It was not long before the new arrivals became acquainted with the sublime flavour of the Sydney rock oyster and native flat oysters that grew wild in all the estuaries and river entrances along the east coast. Australians embraced the ocean and its denizens with increasing enthusiasm. Nowadays over 3.5 million Australians fish recreationally, and most enjoy a seafood meal at least once a week. Over 90 per cent of Australians eat seafood.

While the oceans nourish our souls, threaten us, protect us and define our national identity, they are also home to an astonishing variety of marine flora and fauna. One of the most satisfying culinary pursuits is to catch, prepare and eat absolutely fresh seafood. Whether waist-deep in water, shucking and eating oysters you have just picked off the rocks, or throwing a fillet of freshly caught garfish into a frypan on the back of a boat, whether your fish came from a line thrown from a jetty or you are racing home from the fish market with a bag of fresh sardines, you are doing what so many Australians do—enjoying fresh seafood. The recipes and stories in this book are a celebration of Australia, our maritime history, our oceans and the wonderful seafood they provide.

PURCHASING SEAFOOD

Rarely is the maxim caveat emptor (let the buyer beware) more applicable than when buying seafood. However, by understanding a few principles and following a few rules, anyone can step up to the counter and order with confidence. The trouble with seafood is simply that it goes off quickly. Fresh fish is sublime. Stale fish is revolting.

When I was young, an oft-quoted platitude was never order fish further than 50 miles from the coast. Modern refrigeration and refrigerated transportation has put paid to that.

To further confuse matters nowadays, just because there is a fishing fleet in town doesn't mean the 'fresh' fish in the fish shop came off a local boat. A lot of commercially harvested seafood is snap-frozen at sea at extremely low temperatures. With modern distribution, chances are the fish you order in the harbour town will have come from interstate or overseas.

I like buying fish in the open-air markets of South-East Asia. In the tropics, without refrigeration, the fish has to be absolutely fresh in order to look fresh. Refrigeration prolongs the shelf life of fish but also hides its true age. When buying fish, talk to the fishmonger, pick their brains and most importantly, use your sense and your senses.

There are key indicators when purchasing **whole fish** that will help. Firstly, look at the eyes. They should bulge slightly and be bright and clear. Sunken or cloudy eyes indicate the fish is past its prime. Make sure the fish has a lustrous, bright colour. Check that the gills are pink or scarlet and not brown or grey. If you poke the fish with your finger the flesh should be firm and spring back; if you leave an indentation the fish is old. This can be hard to do in a shop so ask the fishmonger to do it for you. The scales should be firm. Smell is critical. Nothing repels more than the smell of off fish—it should smell of the sea.

Purchasing **filleted fish** requires greater discernment as it is more difficult to tell freshness. The less scrupulous fishmonger will fillet whole fish that has been *in the cabinet a little long* to disguise its age. Fillets should be shiny and firm with a bright colour and good shape. Look carefully for browning around the edges, or yellow discoloration that will indicate age. Stay clear of fillets that ooze water when touched or are sitting in a puddle of liquid. Frozen fillets will not be as bright and shiny but may still be edible. Beware of frozen fish that has been thawed, as the fishmonger is doing you no favours by thawing it. Better you purchase it frozen and thaw it yourself when you are ready to eat it.

When buying **frozen fish** from the deep-freeze, look carefully at the package. There should be no tears or breaches. There should be no dark or white spots—discolouration, or fading in the flesh that could indicate drying out. The flesh should not have ice crystals, which indicates the fish has been stored for a long time, or worse still, thawed and refrozen. Always ensure the package comes from below the frost line.

Mussels and pipis must be cooked live. They should have a fresh sea smell and be firmly closed. They're just like people: if they are lying around with their traps open, it indicates they are dead! Mussels and oysters are indiscriminate filter feeders and readily accumulate toxins, so it is essential that you only eat those harvested from pristine water. Mussels, oysters and other bi-valve molluscs take on the flavour of the environment they are grown in, including the surrounding marine flora, the geology of the seabed and the algae in the water.

Oysters should have their traps loosely closed and when disturbed they should shut tightly. I avoid eating oysters in January and February as the warmer waters induce them to convert their fat content to spawn, becoming milky and creamy. They come back to good condition in mid to late March. Preferably buy your oysters straight out of the hessian bag they came in, unshucked. If you find the task of shucking formidable, get your fishmonger to do it for you. Avoid buying opened oysters if possible as their age could be questionable and they are likely to have been 'plumped', a procedure where the foot that secures them to the shell is severed and the oyster is washed then returned to the shell upside-down, resulting in a deceased oyster and the loss of their delicious liquor. While saltier, they are much better 'topless' with just the top shell removed and the foot and liquor still intact. If you must buy them opened, ensure they are glossy, firm, moist and have a fresh smell.

Scallops are best consumed within 36 hours of purchase, and should be purchased 'dry', which means off the shell. The flesh should be off-white or light brown and the roe red. When scallops are 'wet' they are white and have been soaked to increase their weight (they will absorb up to 45 per cent of their weight in water). This unscrupulous practice is profitable for the fishmonger but disastrous for the cook and the consumer. Be warned!

A live **rock lobster** or crayfish is called 'green' regardless of the colour, and should flap its tail like crazy when handled. Do not buy dead green lobster unless they are tails that have been snap-frozen. Lobster can be bought pre-boiled, where it is bright red and its tail should be curled tightly against its body. If the tail is not curled, the lobster was more than likely already dead when it was boiled and will not be good eating. Lobster should always feel heavy for its size when you pick it up, and should smell sweet and never of ammonia. It is best eaten as soon as possible.

Mud crabs will have their claws tied when you purchase them—so they don't remove your fingers when handled! They should show plenty of leg movement and their eyes should be alert, darting around. This goes for all live crab. If the crab is not live, ensure it smells clean and fresh and the shell is unbroken and has a glossy appearance.

Prawns are available either green (uncooked) or cooked. I never buy cooked prawns as I have always been disappointed with the taste and texture. I prefer to cook fresh or frozen green prawns. Never buy green prawns that have black heads or are oozing black fluid. They should smell sweet without any scent of ammonia and should not be sweaty. Remember that buying whole prawns yields half their weight in meat once the heads and shells are removed.

Cuts of seafood and market terminology
Fish
Whole Whole fish with gut in

GG Whole fish gutted and gilled

HG Whole fish gutted with the head removed

Butterflied Fish gutted, boned and split flat with the head on

Butterflied fillets Fish gutted, boned and split flat with the head removed

Fillets Skin and rib bones removed

S & B fillets Skin, rib and pin bones removed

Portions S & B fillets cut into pieces

Skin-on fillets Fillets with rib bones removed, skin left on

Cutlets Fish cut in thick cross-sections

Steaks Portions of fillets from large fish such as tuna without skin

Butchered fillets Fillets with the rib bones, wing and skin left on

Prawns
Green Raw, unprocessed

Cutlets Head and shell removed, tail intact

Meat Head and shell removed

Tail Shell-on tails

WC Whole, cooked, with shell and head on

A rough guide to buying quantities
Whole fish 500 g (1 lb 2 oz) per person

Fillet 250 g (9 oz) per person

Prawns 6–8 large prawns per person as part of a main dish

Whole crabs 500–700 g (1 lb – 1 lb 9 oz) per person; around 25 per cent of a crab is edible flesh

Whole lobster 500 g – 1 kg (1–2 lb) per person

Mussels 12–18 per person

Scallops 6 as a first course, 12 for a main

Crab, prawn, lobster, scallop or squid meat 150 g (5 oz) per person

Storing seafood

As a rough guide, always eat fresh seafood within two days of purchase. Don't leave it unrefrigerated for long, especially in a hot car. If you are shopping, take an esky or a car refrigerator with you, or ask the fishmonger to pack the fish in crushed ice. Be careful when handling seafood. Bruised seafood spoils more readily.

On getting your **fish** home, unwrap it, rinse it in cold water and pat it dry with paper towel. Ideally, place a wire rack and some ice blocks in a baking tray and place the fish on the rack and cover with cling wrap. Do not let the fish come in direct contact with the ice as it 'burns' and detracts from the flavour. If fish sits in its own juices on a plate it deteriorates rapidly. Store it as close to 0°C (32°F) as possible.

If you are not going to eat it soon, freeze it immediately, although unfortunately, home freezers don't snap-freeze, so thawed fish will never be as good as when it was fresh. Rinse the fish and pat it dry. Put it in a freezer bag, expel all the air, seal, label, date and deep-freeze. Some people like to glaze the fish with a brine prior to freezing to prevent freezer burn. If your refrigerator can maintain a temperature of -18°C (0°F) or lower, your frozen fish will last 9–12 months. Fatty fish such as mullet will have a shorter life of around 3–4 months. When thawing, always thaw in the refrigerator to stop the growth of food-poisoning bacteria and to preserve taste, smell and texture. If you must thaw fillets of fish quickly, do so in cold water with enough sea salt added to resemble sea water (35 g per litre or 1 ¼ oz per 2 pints). The salt will inhibit osmosis, preventing the water being taken up by the cells of the fish, thereby preventing the fish from becoming mushy.

Store live **oysters, mussels and pipis** in a cool place out of direct sunlight in a damp hessian bag. Pacific oysters will last around a week at 4°C (39°F) unshucked, while Sydney rock oysters have a longer shelf life, lasting up to three weeks at temperatures up to 10°C (50°F). Do not immerse them in fresh water or you will drown them. Do not place them in airtight containers or you will suffocate them. Do not place them on ice or they die of cold.

Live lobster can be wrapped in damp paper and stored in the refrigerator, where it will live for 24 hours.

Smoked fish can be stored in an airtight container or wrapped in foil or greaseproof paper in the refrigerator. Do not wrap smoked fish in cling wrap as it sweats.

Ethical considerations

I didn't spend millions of years evolving to the top of the food chain to become a vegetarian. I love all kinds of seafood, but as the world's fishing grounds face increasing pressure from commercial and recreational fishing, there are ethics and sustainability issues we need to consider when purchasing seafood. Which fish populations are healthy and which are in decline? Where was the fish caught? For example, snapper populations are healthy in Australian waters but seriously depleted in New Zealand waters. Think about the water quality where the fish was caught. Consider how it was caught. Non-selective fishing methods like trawl-netting and long-line fishing kill non-targeted species like turtle and dolphin. About one-quarter of the global fish catch is bycatch!

Buy lower down the food chain. The populations of large predators like shark and bluefin tuna have been in steady decline, have higher levels of mercury and require more energy to process.

The speed with which fish reproduce can be critical for their survival as a species. Quick-growing and fast-spawning seafood like anchovies and oysters would be better choices for frequent consumption than shark, Patagonian toothfish and orange roughy. I am not advocating or suggesting you never eat species higher up the food chain, just that it will be better for both you and the oceans to choose lower species more frequently.

Seafood raised by aquaculture now accounts for almost half the seafood consumed worldwide. While this relieves pressure on wild fish populations, it comes with its own associated problems, such as the antibiotics and parasiticides used being dispersed into the ocean and disrupting ecosystems. Often more weight in wild fish is required to create fishmeal feed than the weight of fish the farm produces, resulting in a net loss of protein from the sea. Shrimp farms in South-East Asia have contributed to the destruction of mangrove habitats, and concerns have been raised regarding salmonella levels as chicken manure is reportedly used as a fertiliser in tropical ponds.

COOKING SEAFOOD

Fish is easy to cook. It is quick, good for you, tasty, and takes on numerous flavours and textures ... but ... undercook it and it will be pink and sticky, overcook it and it will be dry and flaky. It is unforgiving. To get a better idea of why this is, a little science comes in handy.

Beef is red because cows' muscles use a lot of oxygen and therefore have high myoglobin content, containing iron and oxygen. Fish don't use as much energy, they float in less gravity and generally get about with the flick of a tail, so therefore they don't have high myoglobin, which makes their meat light and translucent. During the process of cooking fish, the proteins denature or unwind and then reattach, or coagulate, whereby the molecules shrink and water is squeezed out. This makes the fish opaque, as light cannot pass through the coagulated proteins. Take a fork and gently prise back the fish at its thickest part and check that the flesh has lost its translucent appearance and is opaque all the way through. As a general practice, it is best to slightly undercook fish as it will continue cooking once off the heat. By the time it reaches the table it will be cooked through.

Poaching

To poach a large fish like a whole Atlantic salmon, you need a fish kettle—a long, narrow saucepan that fits large whole fish, with a perforated layer that can be lifted out. If this is not available, wrap the fish in muslin and tie it at each end so you can remove the fish without it breaking up. Smaller fish can be poached in deep frying pans or baking dishes either on the stovetop or in the oven. If the fish is not completely submerged, you can place celery leaves over the top to prevent it from drying out. Fish can be poached in water, salt water, milk or, most commonly, court bouillon or fish stock. The fish is usually immersed in cold poaching liquid and brought up to a simmer. This prevents the skin from bursting. Fish should never be rapidly boiled as this makes the flesh break up and become watery. Always drain the fish well before serving so as not to drown or spoil the accompaniments. Poaching times vary according to the fish, but the following rough guides apply:

- **Large whole fish up to around 3 kg (6 lb 10 oz)** 15–20 minutes per kilogram.
- **Small whole fish such as whiting** 15–20 minutes. The appearance of the fish should indicate when it is cooked. The eyes should be white and the flesh should be opaque all the way through.
- **Fillets** 8–12 minutes.
- **Cutlets** 10–20 minutes. When the bone can easily be detached from the meat, the fish is cooked. In the case of salmon it is considered optimal to cook it a little underdone.

Grilling

I love grilling fish. Ideal for grilling are oily or moist fish like sardines, flounder, ling, tailor, perch, sole or bream. Do not grill fillets without the skin, and likewise any soft fish that may break up. If you are grilling whole, plump fish, make a few diagonal slits in the sides to allow the heat through to the thicker parts of the flesh. The gut cavity of whole fish can be stuffed and sewn up before grilling. Make sure the grill is hot and brush the fish with a little oil beforehand. On an open fire, do not grill on a naked flame, but allow the flames to die down to embers. A hinged fish rack can be a handy device for ease of turning. Fillets of fish will normally take somewhere between 2–5 minutes to grill. Anchovy butter (page 187) goes well with grilled fish. Place a dab on the fish when it comes off the grill.

Deep-frying

A very flavoursome way to cook all kinds of fish. For details on technique, see the recipe for fish and chips on pages 119–20.

Pan-frying

Pan-frying is a lovely way to cook fish. I love flathead tails (especially fried in butter), King George whiting, sweet fillets from the prickly gurnard, or the wonderful little garfish that fight like miniature marlin on a light tackle. The standard method is to fry on a stovetop in a heavy cast-iron or non-stick pan. Butter, ghee or olive oil is generally the medium. The fish is lightly dusted in flour or crumbed, and then fried, turning once. One technique of frying delicate flesh like whiting or garfish is *à la meunière*, where the fish is dusted in flour, gently fried in oil or clarified butter, and traditionally served on an oval plate with lemon juice, a little more butter and some chopped parsley. Thick pieces of tuna or salmon are often marinated in a little olive oil and seared in a very hot pan and served rare, like a steak. In North Africa, fish is often fried in a pan and then buried in a sauce to finish like a stew.

Stir-frying

This is a great healthy way to cook scallops, squid or marinara mix with vegetables. Ideally, use a wok burner on a stovetop that can achieve very high heat, have all your ingredients ready to go, heat the wok to hot and stir like crazy! When stir-frying fish, use a firm variety. Rather than heating your wok to blistering, fry the fish gently first, then remove it and put some serious heat under the wok to vigorously fry the vegetables. Return the fish to the wok at the end, thereby keeping the fish intact.

Steaming

I would be lost without my bamboo steamers. Put a wok on the stove, fill the base with water and place the bamboo steamer over the top. The water should be at a rolling boil to produce plenty of steam. Inside a large steamer you can place a whole fish on a plate, or on leaves. A whole fish of 800 g (1 lb 12 oz) will take around 15 minutes. You can stack bamboo steamers on top of each other and do multiple steams at once. Bamboo steamers can also sit on top of conventional pots and saucepans.

Baking

In its most basic form, fish can be baked by placing it on a lightly oiled baking tray, covering it with foil and cooking at 180°C (350°F) until done. For crispy skin, remove the foil for the last few minutes. The fish cavity can be stuffed, or tomatoes, onions, olives and wine can be added to the tray. Fish cooked in a wood-fired pizza oven is delicious.

The French do fillets of fish *en papillotes*, where a dollop of thick cream is placed in the centre of a piece of greaseproof paper. A small fish or a fillet is placed on top with a little more cream and seasoning and some chopped herbs. The paper is folded tightly and the parcel is baked in a very hot oven for around 15 minutes.

Seasoned fish can be wrapped in leaves, paperbark or foil and baked in the oven or in the coals of the campfire. Fish can also be caked in clay and baked in the coals, the clay then smashed with a hammer to reveal a delicious moist fish with a distinct earthy flavour. This technique was popular during Roman times.

SOUPS

Fish stock

This is a basic fish stock. You can add all kinds of things to the recipe: mushrooms, tomatoes, sliced fennel or fennel seeds, saffron. You can also use white wine instead of vermouth.

1 kg (2 lb 3 oz) fish bones and heads
2 shallots, chopped
1 onion, chopped
1 carrot, chopped
1 leek, chopped
1 celery stalk, chopped
2 tablespoons butter
2 cups Noilly Prat dry vermouth
½ lemon, peeled and segmented
3 flat-leaf parsley stalks
large sprig of thyme
1 bay leaf
1 teaspoon salt
1 teaspoon white peppercorns, cracked

Clean the fish bones and heads, ensuring there is no blood as this makes the stock bitter.

Sweat all the vegetables in the butter in a pot until soft. Pour in the vermouth and evaporate by a third, cooking off the alcohol. Add 1.5 litres (3 pints) of cold water and the lemon segments and herbs. Bring to boil and simmer for 20 minutes, skimming several times. Add the salt and pepper in the last 5 minutes. Turn off the heat and allow to steep for 1 hour.

Strain through a sieve and then through muslin cloth. Use immediately or freeze.

Court bouillon

This is not a soup to be eaten, but rather a spiced, aromatic liquor commonly used to poach fish. Court bouillon can be reused provided it is kept refrigerated in a sterilised jar. The simplest version is court bouillon *eau de sel*, which is simply 15 grams (½ oz) of salt to every 1 litre (2 pints) of water.

2 onions, sliced
500 g (1 lb 2 oz) carrots, sliced
sprig of thyme
1 bay leaf
1 tablespoon salt
1 cup cider vinegar
1 bunch flat-leaf parsley
12 black peppercorns

Place the ingredients in a pot except the peppercorns. Add 2 litres (4 pints) of water and simmer for 1 hour. In the last 10 minutes, add the peppercorns. Strain and cool before using or refrigerating.

Bouillabaisse

In great cauldrons on the beach, the fishermen of Marseilles would boil up fish deemed unsuitable for market, particularly the grotesque scorpion fish. Bouillabaisse is the combination of two words, *bouille* (to boil) and *abaisser* (to reduce) and is more a technique than a recipe, but over the years it has become the apotheosis of fish soup. It should be prepared using freshly caught rockfish and shellfish.

To omit a bouillabaisse recipe in a seafood cookbook would be to my mind a great disservice to Australian fish, and this recipe is an Australian no-nonsense version of the traditional. It is flavoured with vegetables, herbs, saffron, pernod and dried orange rind (simply dry orange peel alongside your socks on the heater; what you don't cook makes a great fire starter). You may like to serve this with rouille, a flavoured mayonnaise (page 191).

1 kg (2 lb 3 oz) snapper fillets
1 kg (2 lb 3 oz) flathead tails
750 g (1 lb 10 oz) green prawns
250 g (9 oz) mussel meat
2 onions, chopped
1 leek, chopped
3 tomatoes, chopped
4 garlic cloves, crushed
2 sprigs of fennel tops
1 small bunch flat-leaf parsley
sprig of thyme
1 bay leaf
quarter of dried orange rind
¾ cup extra-virgin olive oil
1 cup dry white wine
generous pinch of saffron threads
salt and cracked pepper
2–3 litres (4–6 pints) fish stock
    (page 2)
2 tablespoons pernod
roughly chopped flat-leaf parsley
slices of dry bread

Place all the ingredients except the pernod in a large pot, pouring in enough fish stock to cover the fish. Marinate in the refrigerator overnight.

Gently bring to the boil, then reduce the heat and simmer for 20 minutes. Remove the fish and shellfish to a bowl. Strain the liquid through a sieve lined with muslin. Stir in the pernod.

Come and get it

Line a soup tureen with the dry bread. Pour in the hot soup and sprinkle with some of the chopped parsley. Place the warm fish and shellfish in a separate bowl and sprinkle with more parsley. Take to the table and serve.

New England clam chowder

According to New England food historian, chef and author Jasper White in his book *50 Chowders*, the earliest known printed recipe for chowder appeared in the *Boston Evening Post* on 23 September 1751. It read:

> First lay some onions to keep the pork from burning
> Because in chouder there can be not turning;
> Then lay some pork in slices very thin,
> Thus you in chouder always must begin.
> Next lay some fish cut crossways very nice
> Then season well with pepper, salt, and spice;
> Parsley, sweet marjoram, savory, and thyme,
> Then biscuit next which must be soak'd some time.
> Thus your foundation laid, you will be able
> To raise a chouder, high as Tower of Babel;
> For by repeating o'er the same again,
> You may make a chouder for a thousand men.
> Last a bottle of claret, with water eno' to smother 'em,
> You'll have a mess which some call omnium gather 'em.

New Englanders use native American clams, which they call quahogs. In Australia we have wonderful Goolwa cockles from South Australia that make an excellent but unconventional substitute.

2 kg (4 lb 6 oz) Goolwa or other
    cockles or pipis
2 boiled potatoes, peeled and diced
1 teaspoon extra-virgin olive oil
2 rashers salty bacon
1 teaspoon butter
1 onion, finely chopped
2 garlic cloves, finely chopped
sprig each of thyme, flat-leaf
    parsley, oregano, rosemary and
    tarragon, leaves finely chopped
1 bay leaf
1 cup cream
1 cup milk
salt and cracked white pepper
extra chopped flat-leaf parsley
    to serve

Soak the cockles in sea water, or water with sea salt added at 35 g (1 ¼ oz) per litre (2 pints), for 1 hour. Vigorously knock the container every so often—this causes them to release any sand or grit.

In a large heavy-based saucepan with a tight-fitting lid, bring 2 cups of water to the boil and add the cockles. Put the lid on and boil for 5 minutes. Stir, then cook for another 3–4 minutes. Strain the cockles and return the broth to the saucepan (about 4 cups). Add the diced potato. When the cockles are cool, shell and set aside.

Gently heat the olive oil in a heavy-based frying pan. Add the bacon and fry slowly to render the fat. Once rendered, increase the heat and crisp the bacon. Drain on paper towel.

Wipe out the pan and add the butter, onion, garlic and herbs. Gently sauté until the onion is soft but not browned. Add to the cockle broth. Boil rapidly for a few minutes to thicken, then reduce to a very slow simmer. Add the cockles, cream and milk. Heat gently without boiling, stirring well. Season to taste and remove the bay leaf.

Come and get it
Ladle the soup into bowls and garnish with parsley. Break the bacon in small pieces over the top.

Mutiny and Massacre
The Batavia and Her Miscreant Supercargo

The insatiable European appetite for spice generated incalculable wealth for the worthy members of the Dutch East India Company. A fleet sailed from Amsterdam on 27 October 1628 bound for the East Indies with the brand new *Batavia* as its flagship. Her skipper was Adriaen Jacobsz, a drunk and a womaniser who harboured enmity against the fleet commodore, François Pelsaert. Her under merchant, or supercargo, was Jeronimus Cornelisz, a thirty-year-old apothecary from Haarlem who may have been fleeing bankruptcy and possibly charges of heresy. As the voyage progressed he began to hatch a plan with Jacobsz to steal the *Batavia* and engage in piracy on the high seas.

After leaving Cape Town, the fleet was separated in bad weather. Not having longitude, the Dutch skippers were instructed to chart a course across the Indian Ocean until they sighted the coast of the great unnamed southern continent, where they would swing north and head for the port of Batavia on Java.

On 4 June 1629, in the early hours before dawn, the *Batavia* smashed into the Morning Reef in the Houtman Abrolhos, a group of low-lying islands of coral rubble 50 miles off today's town of Geraldton on the Western Australian coast. Four days later, Pelsaert, together with the ship's officers, some of the crew and some passengers, left 268 castaways on the wreck and on two small barren islands and went in the ship's 300-foot longboat in search of water. Finding none, they headed north along the rocky desert coast. At one point they startled a group of Aboriginals, who fled at full speed. Pelsaert recorded, 'They were black savages, quite naked, leaving themselves uncovered like animals'. In a remarkable feat of navigation, they successfully made it to Batavia in thirty-three days. Jacobsz was immediately arrested for negligence and the boatswain executed for outrageous behaviour before the loss of the ship.

Pelsaert was granted the ship *Saerdam* by Governor-General Jan Pietersz Coen to recover the *Batavia* castaways. Promptly victualled and replete with a team of Indian divers to recover the lost treasure aboard the *Batavia*, Pelsaert sailed on 15 July. Contrary winds and bad luck combined, meaning that the *Saerdam* took sixty-three days to relocate the wreck site.

Meanwhile, on the Houtman Abrolhos, Cornelisz, as the most senior member of the company, had taken control. He hatched a plan to hijack any rescue ship that appeared. But first he decided that he had to reduce the survivors' numbers to around forty. He removed the group of twenty loyal soldiers under the command of a Lieutenant Wiebbe Hayes, including six Frenchmen, to West Wallabi and marooned them there. They were instructed to find water but were not expected to find any. He then coerced a group of mutineers to sign a contract of loyalty. And with this, a *grand guignol* of murder and mayhem was unleashed on the remaining loyal castaways. The sick were the first to go, eleven in number. Andreas de Vries was ordered to go into the hospital hut and cut their throats, which he did. The minister was invited to dine with Cornelisz while his wife and five of his six daughters were done away with, after which Cornelisz muttered, 'The Parson won't live long either'. The Provost and fourteen of his men were thrown into the sea. Four swam to safety only to be put to the sword. Anries Jonasz thrust a pike through Paulus Barentsz and then cut the throat of the pregnant May Soets. Andries de Bruyn the cabin boy was sent to catch some birds. Allert Jansz was sent after him to cut his throat. The little boat was sent to Seal's Island to dispatch all the people there. Cornelisz handed Jan Hendricksz his dagger saying, 'Go and cut out the heart of Stoffel Stoffelsz, that lazy butt, who stands there working as if his back was broken'. To Jan van Bommel he gave his sword saying, 'Go and try whether it is sharp enough; cut off the head of Coen Aldertsz with it'. The steward Jan Pillegronsz de Bye, eighteen years of age, murdered women and children but broke down and cried when permission to cut off the head of Cornelisz Aldersz was refused. The butchery went on and on. Men, women and children were slaughtered. When most of the murdering was done, Cornelisz distributed the remaining women as booty. The widow Lucretia Jans he took for himself.

Intoxicated with power, Cornelisz had costumes of scarlet made up from the ship's stores to clothe himself and his deputies, 'trimming them with so much gold lace that the material was hardly visible'. Cornelisz also dressed himself in silk stockings and garters with gold trimmings. He must have cut a dazzling swathe through the stark white sand and low-lying scrub of the barren island they had named Batavia's Graveyard.

Against the odds, Hayes and his men had survived on West Wallabi Island. They had found wallabies aplenty, and, incredibly, after twenty days of searching they had finally found water. Amid the mayhem on the other islands, a boatswain's mate, Pieter Lambertsz, had managed to construct a little boat and slip away to West Wallabi. Another group stole a boat and also escaped; it included Lucas the bottler's mate, Cornelis the fat trumpeter, deaf Jan Michielsz and squinting Heyndrick. Hayes' group of loyalists had now grown to forty-seven. Cornelisz next focused his attentions on these survivors. A boat with twenty-two mutineers was sent to attack them, but Hayes and his men repelled it, knee-deep in water. The following day, three boats with thirty-seven men tried again. A ceasefire was brokered by the minister, but the next day Hayes captured Cornelisz and put four of his deputies to the sword.

A day later, Pelsaert, aboard the *Saerdam*, sighted the Houtman Abrolhos. On 17 September the commodore went ashore on one of the islands after seeing smoke and to his surprise found it abandoned. At this point, an excited Hayes rowed around the headland. After briefing Pelsaert he urged him to go back on board, as the mutineers were planning to take the ship. Sure enough, a boatload of armed red-and-gold-bedecked miscreants was headed in their direction. Without a struggle they were taken and put in irons. Hayes took the prisoner Cornelisz on board that evening.

Over the next two weeks, the mutineers were put to the wheel and water boarded to extract their testimonies. The horror of what had taken place began to unfold. Pelsaert decided to pass sentence on the ringleaders then and there, rather than run the risk of their evil polluting the ship en route back to Java. On 1 October, Cornelisz was taken to Seal's Island, where both his hands were cut off and he was hung from the gallows that had been erected. Seven others joined him at the gallows after having their right hands severed. Nine further mutineers were transported back to Batavia, keelhauled, hung from the yardarms and beaten along the way.

The *Batavia* incident was responsible for a number of Australian firsts. The first European structure on Australian soil was a stone fortress built by Hayes, the walls of which are still standing on West Wallabi Island. Two mutineers put ashore on the mainland were Australia's first European residents. The trial and subsequent executions of the mutineers were the first European judicial trial and corporal sentence. The story serves as a reminder that a ship at sea, particularly one reliant on nature, can be seen as a microcosm of the greater human society. It is disturbing to think how easily it can fall apart.

Prawn bisque

This is a classic thick and creamy French soup based on the famous *bisque d'homard*—lobster soup. You can substitute any crustacean: crab, rock lobster, Moreton Bay bugs, even yabbies. The bisque extracts every bit of flavour from the crustaceans, including the shells, resulting in a delicious essence. The recipe is long but each step is reasonably simple; the end product is a messy kitchen and a great soup!

120 g (4 oz) unsalted butter
1 onion, finely chopped
½ carrot, finely chopped
½ celery stalk, finely chopped
2 garlic cloves, crushed
1 kg (2 lb 3 oz) green prawns
⅓ cup cognac
1 tablespoon tomato paste
1 bay leaf
1 tablespoon tarragon leaves
pinch of cayenne
200 ml (7 fl oz) dry white wine
3 cups fish stock (page 2)
½ cup thick cream
chopped flat-leaf parsley

Melt half of the butter in a heavy-based saucepan. Add the onion, carrot and celery (a combination of vegetables the French call *mirepoix*), and garlic, and cook for 5 minutes or so until the vegetables are soft.

Add the prawns and cook over medium heat for around 5 minutes until the shells are pink. Turn the heat up very high. When hot, carefully add the cognac. It should flame; if not, put a match to it. Once the flames have died, stir in the tomato paste, bay leaf, tarragon, cayenne and wine. Boil until the wine is almost completely evaporated.

Add 2 cups of the fish stock, cover the saucepan with a lid and cook gently for 30 minutes, shaking the pan occasionally. Strain the broth into a bowl, then wipe out the saucepan and return the broth to it.

Reserve 8 prawns and place the rest of the solids in a blender with a little of the broth and pulse to a coarse purée. Strain through muslin back into the broth and set aside. Reserve the prawn mash in the muslin.

Melt the remaining butter in a separate saucepan and add the prawn mash as well as four of the reserved prawns and sauté over high heat for 2–3 minutes. Let the mixture cool slightly, then place in the blender and pulse until smooth. Sieve through clean muslin into a bowl and refrigerate to set. Cut into cubes.

Come and get it

Add the remaining stock to the saucepan of broth and heat gently, whisking in the cream. Remove from the heat and stir in the prawn butter 1 cube at a time.

Ladle the bisque into handled soup cups set upon saucers, or into mugs. Top with the remaining reserved prawns and sprinkle with parsley.

Serves 4

Scallop and lemongrass soup

2 tablespoons peanut oil
2 garlic cloves, finely chopped
1 cm (⅓ in) ginger, finely chopped
small red chillies to taste, finely chopped
2 spring onions (scallions), white part only, finely chopped
1 litre (2 pints) fish stock (page 2)
1 lemongrass stalk, finely chopped
250 g (9 oz) scallops with roe, washed and patted dry
fish sauce
coriander (cilantro) leaves
fried shallots

Heat the oil in a heavy-based pot and sauté the garlic, ginger and chilli until fragrant. Add the spring onions and sauté until wilted, then add the stock and lemongrass. Cover with a lid and simmer for 45 minutes.

Strain the broth through a fine sieve and return to the heat. Bring to a gentle boil then add the scallops and cook for 1 minute. Add fish sauce to taste, 1 teaspoon at a time, stirring after each addition.

Come and get it
Remove scallops with a slotted spoon and place in bowls. Ladle the broth on top and sprinkle with coriander and fried shallots.

Hot and sour prawn soup (*Tom yum goong*)

Of all the seafood broths in the world, Thailand's *tom yum* is a standout. Its distinctive hot and sour flavour and generous use of fragrant herbs has made it a favourite around the world. *Tom yum goong* uses prawns, but *tom yum gai* uses chicken, *tom yum pla* uses fish, and *tom yum talay* uses mixed seafood. While each region of Thailand has its own version, they all share the hot and sour theme with a strong citrus undercurrent. For a richer soup, use fish stock instead of water.

8 large green prawns
2 lemongrass stalks
4 garlic cloves, smashed with the skin on
4 shallots, smashed with the skin on
4 slices of fresh or dried galangal
small green chillies to taste, sliced
½ cup tinned straw mushrooms
¼ cup fish sauce, or to taste
½ cup lime juice
1 teaspoon Thai chilli paste (see Glossary, page 248)
handful of coriander (cilantro) leaves

Place the prawns and 1 litre (2 pints) of water in a pot and bring to the boil. Once boiling, remove the prawns and set aside.

Beat the lemongrass stalks with the back of a knife or cleaver and tie each in a knot. Add to the pot together with the garlic, shallots, galangal, chilli and mushrooms. Simmer for 3–4 minutes.

Return the prawns to the pot and add the fish sauce, lime juice and chilli paste. Remove from the heat. Stir well and take out the lemongrass.

Come and get it
Ladle the soup into bowls, dividing the prawns evenly, and garnish generously with coriander.

Bungaree
Australia's First Aboriginal Circumnavigator

> There are few old Australian colonists to whom the name of Bungaree is not familiar; but I conceive it right that the whole world should know something of this departed monarch.
>
> Charles Dickens, *All the Year Round*, vol. 1, April–October 1859

Matthew Flinders wrote his name as 'Bongaree'; Phillip Parker King spelt it 'Boongaree'; and Lachlan Macquarie called him 'Bungaree', which is now the generally accepted spelling. Regardless of how his name was spelt or misspelt, alongside Pemulwuy and Bennelong, he remains one of the three most famous Aboriginal Australians of the nineteenth century. Bennelong was the hapless interlocutor between the Eora people and the British, and sailed to England with Governor Phillip in 1792. Pemulwuy was perhaps Australia's first Indigenous resistance fighter, who was finally killed. Only his head went to England, in a pickle jar. Bungaree was the first Aboriginal to circumnavigate the continent and the subject of no fewer than seventeen known portraits (most governors sat for only two or three).

Bungaree, like Bennelong, was a member of the Eora people, and lived at Broken Bay at the mouth of the Hawkesbury River. Dispossessed by expanding European settlement, he gravitated south together with the remnants of his clan to the settlement of Sydney Cove. In July 1799 he accompanied Matthew Flinders in the *Norfolk* on a coastal survey of Moreton and Hervey bays as a guide and interpreter. Flinders wrote that he had been attracted to Bungaree's 'good disposition and manly conduct'.

In an essay written in tribute to his beloved cat Trim, Flinders recounted how Bungaree and Trim

> formed an intimate acquaintance. If [Trim] had occasion to drink, he mewed to Bongaree and leapt up onto the water cask; if to eat he called him down below and went straight to his kid, where there was generally a remnant of black swan. In short, Bongaree was his great resource, and his kindness was repaid with caresses.

Flinders was so taken with Bungaree that he invited him on the 1802–03 expedition in the *Investigator*. Bungaree's task was difficult and dangerous, for he had to negotiate with the various Aboriginal groups they encountered during the journey. This would have required great skills of diplomacy. Flinders wrote that Bungaree 'often stood naked and unarmed between opposing blacks and whites ... the symmetry of his limbs expressing strength and agility'.

With the *Investigator*'s timbers rotting beneath him, Flinders abandoned his survey at the Wessel Islands, north-east of Arnhem Land, and sailed to Timor to re-provision. To escape the monsoon he tracked south down the west coast of Australia, arriving back at Port Jackson in June 1803 and earning Bungaree his distinction of being the first Aboriginal Australian to circumnavigate the continent.

In 1915 Governor Lachlan Macquarie crowned Bungaree 'Chief of the Broken Bay Tribe' in a lavish ceremony on Middle Head, presenting him with a breastplate inscribed 'Bungaree, King of the Blacks' and 15 acres of land at Georges Head complete with huts, tools, livestock and convict mentors. The governor gave Bungaree some packets of seeds and fish-hooks and some time after inquired of him whether the seeds had yet come up. 'Oh, berry well, berry well', exclaimed Bungaree. 'All make come up berry well, except dem fish-hooks; dem no come up yet'. In mocking himself, his humour typically mocked the white man.

In 1817 Bungaree put to sea again, aboard the *Mermaid* with Phillip Parker King's expedition to survey those sections of north-west Australia not completed previously by Flinders. Flinders and King both praised

his calmness and bravery, his ability to find drinking water and his adeptness at spearing fish to supplement the meagre rations on board. In 1818 he sailed south to Van Diemen's Land, where King charted the entrance to Macquarie Harbour, unlocking Hells Gates, as it was later christened by the hapless convicts who sailed through it.

Bungaree's sense of humour and gift of mimicry were well known. He befriended four governors, and could imitate their movements and idiosyncrasies with astonishing accuracy. He became one of the more colourful characters on the streets of Sydney, usually bedecked in a discarded military uniform. As 'King' he would formally greet ships arriving in the harbour. One contemporary account recorded:

> Bungaree makes one measured stride from the gangway; then turning around the quarter deck lifts his beaver with his right hand a full foot from his head (with all the grace and ease of a court exquisite) and carrying it slowly and solemnly to a full arm's length lowers it in a gentle and most dignified manner down to the very deck following up this motion by an inflection of the body almost equally profound.

Sadly, Bungaree's buffoonery and facile exhibitionism hid a darker, tragic sadness lurking beneath his public image, and his life descended into one of drunkenness and depravity. One account describes him on board a ship in the harbour waving toward the north shore and proclaiming proudly, 'This is my land'. He then begged for 'tobacco, old clothing, guineas' and left the sloop 'half drunk with awful shouts'. After a long illness, Bungaree died in Sydney in December 1830.

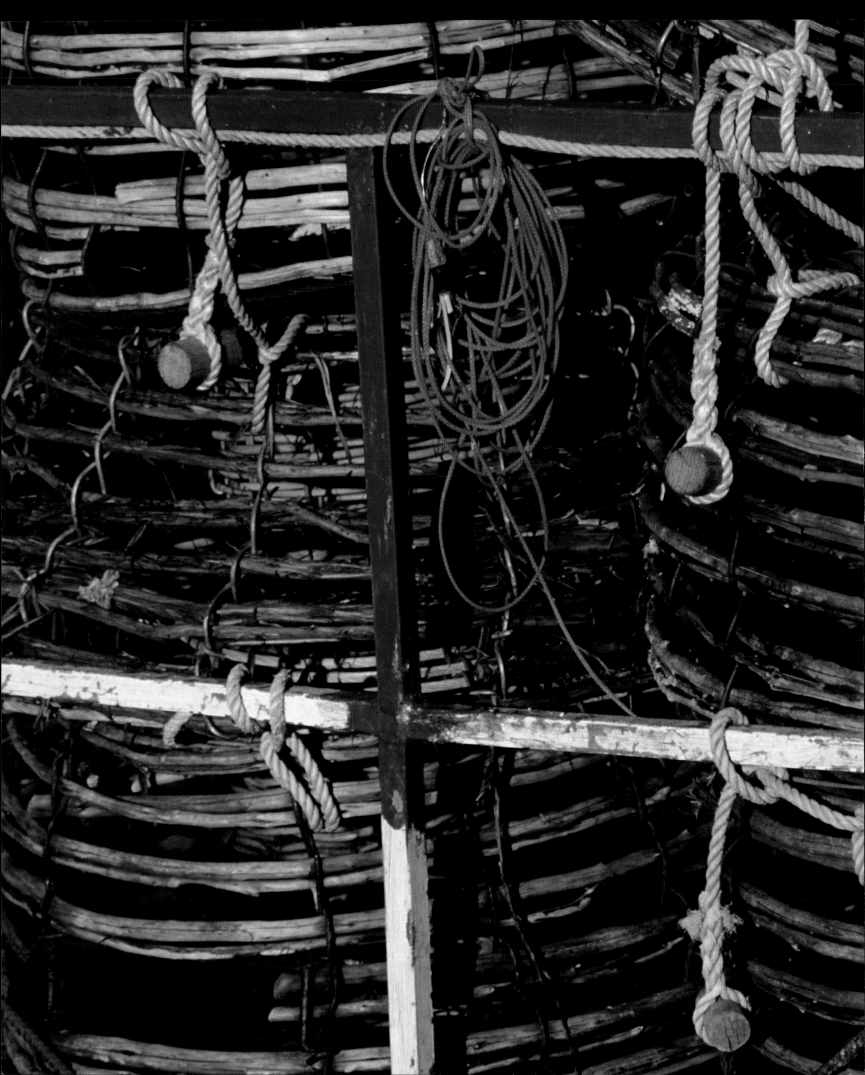

CRUSTACEANS

Blue swimmer crabs with macadamia and wild-lime mayonnaise

Blue swimmer crabs are caught throughout Australia. In fact, they are found in all oceans, being the world's largest commercial catch of crab. While they are sweetest in this recipe, mud crabs or sand crabs also work well. The rare velvet crab that occasionally presents itself in craypots in southern Australia is also excellent.

The wild limes for the mayonnaise can be purchased from bush-foods suppliers, or you could use the flesh and seeds of three native finger limes, which come into season in summer. Failing these, use regular lime. The mayonnaise also incorporates crab 'mustard', the yellow section of the crab's digestive system, which has a delicious but acquired taste (or you can simply use Dijon mustard).

500–700 g (1 lb – 1 lb 9 oz) blue swimmer crab per person

Mayonnaise
2 duck egg yolks
400 ml (13 fl oz) macadamia oil, or olive oil (not extra-virgin)
    if unavailable
10 wild limes or 2 regular limes, juiced
salt
1 teaspoon crab 'mustard' or Dijon mustard

To cook the crabs, bring a large pot of sea water or salted water to the boil. Immerse the crabs and simmer for 5–7 minutes. (In winter, crab shells are thinner and will take less time to cook than in summer.) When the crabs are cooked, take them out of the water and lay them upside-down on a rack to settle for 5 minutes or so. Meanwhile, make the mayonnaise.

Whisk the egg yolks in a bowl (porcelain is ideal). Add about 100 ml (3 ½ fl oz) of the macadamia oil drop by drop until it begins to emulsify. Once emulsified, whisk faster and add the remaining oil in a steady stream. When all the oil is incorporated, add the lime juice and salt to taste. Add the 'mustard' from the crabs or Dijon mustard.

Come and get it
Break the crabs open, dip the meat in the mayonnaise and enjoy!

Crispy banana prawns with spicy salt and piri piri

1 teaspoon Sichuan peppercorns
1 teaspoon cumin seeds
¼ cup salt
24 green banana prawns
1 litre (2 pints) peanut oil
3 limes, cut into wedges
piri piri sauce (page 40)

Put the Sichuan peppercorns and cumin seeds in a heavy-based frying pan and cover with the salt. Heat gently without stirring until the mixture is fragrant and the salt browns slightly. Remove from the heat and allow to cool, then grind in a mortar.

Split the prawns in half lengthwise through their shells and clean. Lay on paper towel to dry.

Heat the oil in a wok to 170°C (340°F). Deep-fry the prawns until crisp. Drain on paper towel.

Come and get it
Toss the prawns in the spicy salt and serve immediately with lime wedges and piri piri sauce.

Seven Weeks in a Leaky Boat
The Journey of the Bounty Launch

The *Bounty* departed from Spithead, England, on 23 December 1787 under the command of Lieutenant William Bligh. Its mission was to sail to Tahiti, take on board a quantity of breadfruit plants and transport them to the West Indies, where they were to be propagated to feed the Negro slaves working the sugar plantations.

Ten months later, on 26 October 1788, the *Bounty* rounded Point Venus and dropped anchor off the palm-fringed black volcanic beach at Matavai Bay. For five blissful months, the crew of the *Bounty* gardened, propagated and prepared the breadfruit for the long sea journey ahead, and fell for the 'sirenian allurements'—the Tahitian women—of whose abundant sexual favours the tars partook with persistent enthusiasm. Finally, on 5 April 1789, the *Bounty* weighed anchor and sailed westward.

On the night of 27 April, Bligh slept as he always did with his door open, in case he was needed on deck. In the grey light of dawn he was seized by a group of sailors led by Lieutenant Fletcher Christian and hauled up onto the deck. With a cutlass in hand, Christian repeatedly threatened to blow Bligh's brains out. Bligh later wrote: 'Of all diabolical looking Men he exceeded every possible description'. The ship's launch was put over the side and Bligh's people were ordered into it. The boatswain and a seaman were allowed to collect twine, canvas, lines, sails, cordage and a 28-gallon cask of water; the carpenter took his tool chest; the captain's clerk fetched a quadrant and compass. Then Christian said, 'Come, Captain Bligh, your officers and men are now in the boat, and you must go with them; if you attempt to make the least resistance you will instantly be put to death'. Bligh was untied and sent over the side into the launch. Four cutlasses and a few pieces of pork were thrown in after him.

Bligh was cast adrift in the middle of the vast Pacific Ocean with eighteen men crammed into a dinghy just 23 feet long and 6 feet wide, with provisions for five days. Above the jeering of the pirates aboard the *Bounty*, Bligh called to the remaining loyalists, 'Never fear, my lads; I'll do you justice if ever I reach England!'

And so began what most naval experts consider the greatest open-boat voyage in maritime history. With a lug rig for a sail, Bligh initially set a course for Tonga, some 50 miles to the west. His navigation was extraordinary: all he had was a broken sextant, a quadrant, a compass and a few basic tables. With no charts, he had to rely on the memory of his trip ten years before, when he had sailed with James Cook. He tied knots in a length of rope and cast it overboard to determine speed, and in the foulest weather navigated across the boundless Pacific, keeping a meticulous log throughout.

At Tonga, after an onshore skirmish with natives that resulted in the stoning to death of one John Norton, Bligh decided not to visit any more islands. Taking stock of his supplies, he determined that to travel the 3600 miles to the nearest European settlement, at Coupang in Dutch Indonesia, they would have to endure starvation rations. He extracted from each man a 'sacred promise' that he would live on one ounce of bread and a quarter-pint of water per day.

The following morning, the sun 'rose very firey and Red, a sure indication of a Severe Gale'. By mid morning the tiny boat was in violent seas. Any unnecessary items were cast overboard, and the men bailed day and night to keep the boat afloat. For weeks they endured torrential rain. Three times daily Bligh doled out the rations, occasionally supplementing them with a teaspoon of rum. The wet weather eventually abated, and instead they suffered under a blistering tropical sun.

One month after the mutiny, the Great Barrier Reef was sighted. Bligh brought the boat through a gap in the breakers and sailed into sheltered waters. He made for a small island just off the coast and, when confident it was uninhabited, beached the boat. The men staggered out of their cramped vessel and onto dry land. They made a hearty stew from oysters and the hearts of palm trees, collected berries and replenished their water.

After two days they sailed north, rounding Cape York on 4 June, once again launching into open ocean. Again they encountered fearsome storms, but, on 15 June, an improvised Jack that Bligh had fashioned from signal flags was sent up the mast—'for I did not choose to land without leave'—and they sailed into Coupang. Received warmly by the Dutch, Bligh was given the only vacant house in the tiny settlement, where he chose to house all his starving, exhausted men.

They recuperated for two months in Coupang, then Bligh purchased a 34-foot schooner and, on 20 August, ran out of the harbour. For six weeks, with the *Bounty*'s launch in tow, Bligh sailed along the coast of Java to the city of Batavia, and from there he took passage to Europe on the *Vlijit*, a Dutch East India vessel bound for Holland. On the evening on 13 March 1790, in a heavy fog, Bligh was dropped on the Isle of Wight, from where he immediately took a ferry to Portsmouth. The following morning he went by post-chaise to London, and, 321 days after the mutiny, arrived at Admiralty House in Pall Mall, ready to give his account and have his revenge.

What led Christian to mutiny is to this day hotly debated among historians. When Bligh was asked his opinion, he simply replied 'Insanity'. Christian was from a well-to-do family; Bligh had taken him on as his protégé, and dined with him on the voyage every few nights. Perhaps it was too difficult for the sailors to return to the hard shipboard life of the British Navy after five months on an idyllic exotic island.

Sautéed lobster tails with whisky and lime

One night in a tin shed on a barley farm at the tip of Yorke Peninsula, South Australia, I was presented with two lobster tails and not much else. On the spur of the moment I turned out this dish and it was sublime.

2 green lobster tails
¼ cup extra-virgin olive oil
3 garlic cloves, chopped
splash of whisky
120 g (4 oz) unsalted butter
1 lime, zested and juiced
salt and cracked pepper

Carefully remove the lobster meat from the shells, being careful to keep the tip of the tail meat intact.

Heat a large heavy-based frying pan until hot. Add the oil, garlic and lobster tails and sauté, turning frequently for 2–3 minutes, until browned.

Add the whisky and stand back—it should flame. If it doesn't, your pan isn't hot enough and you can throw a match to it.

Lower the heat and add the butter and lime zest. Wait for the butter to melt and coat the tails, then stir in the lime juice and season with salt and pepper.

Come and get it
Transfer the tails to a plate and pour over the juices.

Barbecued tiger prawns with basil nam prik

The direct translation of the Thai word *nam prik* is 'chilli water'. Think of it as a fiery relish or dip.

2 tablespoons dried shrimp
4 garlic cloves
3 tablespoons shrimp paste
2 tablespoons palm sugar
small green chillies to taste
1 cup firmly packed sweet basil leaves
2 limes, juiced
2 tablespoons fish sauce
1 kg (2 lb 3 oz) green tiger prawns
extra lime wedges

Soak the shrimp in water for 30 minutes, then drain and rinse.

Thread the peeled garlic cloves onto a skewer and roast over an open flame until oily and coloured. Be careful not to burn them. Form the shrimp paste into a ball, skewer with a fork and toast over the flame until the colour has lightened and it has started smoking. (Or if your paste is too dry to form a ball, wrap it in foil.)

Place the shrimp, garlic, shrimp paste, palm sugar, chilli and basil in a mortar and pound to a paste. Add the lime juice and fish sauce.

Barbecue the prawns on a hot grill for around 5 minutes, until opaque, turning them halfway through. Place in a bowl and toss with the paste.

Come and get it
Serve the prawns with lime wedges, as well as individual plates and finger bowls.

Singapore chilli mud crab

At Singapore's Changi Beach, bustling open-air restaurants have perfected chilli crab, one of Asia's culinary masterpieces. This recipe tastes especially good when wok-fried over an open fire. On the streets of South-East Asia, they burn coconut husks in braziers, although modern Singapore chefs cook on gas. Mud crabs can be trapped in riverine estuaries and mangrove swamps across northern Australia but beware their claws: they can do serious injury.

Every two years I lead an expedition following the ill-fated explorers Burke and Wills from Melbourne to the Gulf of Carpentaria, and it has become a tradition for me to serve this dish as the sun sets at Karumba.

2 kg (4 lb 6 oz) mud crab
½ cup peanut oil
3 garlic cloves, finely chopped
3 cm (1 in) ginger, finely chopped
6 small red chillies, seeded and chopped
1 teaspoon chilli powder
1 teaspoon sugar
4 spring onions (scallions), finely chopped
2 teaspoons cornflour (cornstarch), dissolved in ½ cup water

Crack the shell of the crab down the centre using the back of a heavy cleaver (this will enable you to cut through it). Chop the crab in half. Scoop out the innards from each half, leaving the yellow 'mustard' if you can. Rinse the crab and chop into large pieces. Cut the legs and claws in pieces and crack them with the back of the cleaver to allow flavours to get in.

Heat the oil in a large wok until smoking, then add the crab and stir-fry for about 5 minutes—by this time the shells will be bright red. Drain off the oil then add the garlic, ginger and fresh chillies and fry briefly. Add the chilli powder, sugar and spring onions and fry briefly. Add the cornflour and stir until thick.

Come and get it
Transfer the crab to a bowl and serve with side plates, as well as finger bowls of warm water with slices of lemon.

Crumbed prawns with salsa verde

Salsa verde
½ tablespoon mint leaves
1 small bunch chives
1 ½ tablespoons flat-leaf parsley
2 tablespoons capers in brine, rinsed
4 anchovies in oil, drained
1 garlic clove, roughly chopped
½ teaspoon Dijon mustard
1 ½ teaspoons lemon juice

Prawns
24 large green prawns
½ cup cornflour (cornstarch)
½ cup plain (all-purpose) flour
½ teaspoon bicarbonate of soda
flaky salt and cracked pepper
1 egg
iced water
1 cup Japanese (panko) breadcrumbs
1 litre (2 pints) peanut oil

For the salsa verde, combine the mint, chives, parsley, capers, anchovies and garlic on a board and chop to a paste. Place in a bowl and stir in the mustard and lemon juice.

Shell the prawns, removing the heads but leaving the tips of the tails intact.

Combine the cornflour, plain flour, bicarbonate of soda, salt and pepper in a mixing bowl. Add the egg, then slowly stir in enough iced water to form a smooth, runny batter. Place the breadcrumbs in a separate bowl.

Heat the oil in a wok or large saucepan to 180°C (350°F). When hot, dip the prawns in the batter then dredge them in breadcrumbs. Deep-fry until golden. Remove with a slotted spoon and drain on paper towel.

Come and get it
Place the salsa verde in a dipping bowl and surround it with the prawns. Serve immediately.

Rice-paper rolls with prawns and pork

These rolls are a favourite of my wife Jane and she never fails to order them when we are in a Vietnamese restaurant. For me, they are great summer food—light on the palate. They are also surprisingly easy to make.

Nuoc cham dipping sauce
1 tablespoon sugar
1 small red chilli, seeded and finely chopped
2 tablespoons lime juice
2 tablespoons fish sauce
2 tablespoons rice vinegar
a few coriander (cilantro) leaves to garnish

Rice-paper rolls
12 rice-paper sheets
100 g (3 ½ oz) rice vermicelli
18 small cooked prawns, shelled, heads removed and de-veined,
    halved lengthwise
24 small slices of Chinese barbecued pork, cold
handful of bean sprouts
¼ cup crushed roasted peanuts
24 coriander (cilantro) leaves
12 Vietnamese mint leaves
12 Thai basil leaves

For the dipping sauce, mix the ingredients in a bowl with 2 tablespoons of water and garnish with coriander leaves.

Put the rice-paper sheets in a tray or dish and fill with cold water. Soak until soft (around 5 minutes).

Meanwhile, place the vermicelli in a bowl and cover with boiling water. Soak until soft (around 3 minutes), then drain and refresh under cold water.

Take a sheet of rice paper out of the water and lay on a clean, dry tea towel. Spread about 1 tablespoon of vermicelli in a short horizontal line towards the lower edge of the circle. Put 3 prawn pieces on top, 2 slices of pork, then a few bean sprouts laid lengthwise so they don't puncture the roll when it is rolled up. Sprinkle a thin line of peanuts on the inside of the filling. Top with 2 coriander leaves, 1 Vietnamese mint leaf and 1 Thai basil leaf.

Carefully fold the bottom edge of the rice paper over the filling. Fold in the sides and then carefully roll up to make a neat, firm cylinder. Continue with the rest of the paper and filling.

Come and get it
Neatly stack the rolls on a plate (a square one looks good) and serve alongside the dipping sauce.

The Cape Otway Light

After the calamitous loss of the *Cataraqui*, in 1845, emigrants became reluctant to make the perilous journey to Australia, opting for the safer passage across the Atlantic to America and Canada. Even the Admiralty suggested that until lighthouses were built migrant and convict ships should refrain from navigating Bass Strait. This threatened the prosperity of the colony, and the Legislative Council demanded that lighthouses be built at the western approaches.

Rising 300 feet and jutting south into Bass Strait, Cape Otway was often the first Australian landfall to be seen by mariners inbound from the roaring forties. It was therefore the logical place to build a light station; however, with no nearby harbour or shelter from the ocean, access would have to be by land. Port Phillip superintendant (later governor) Charles Latrobe undertook the task of pioneering a route to the cape, but reaching it by land proved even tougher than by sea.

The Gadabanud, or 'people of the king parrot language', had inhabited the rainforests of the Otway Ranges since the Dreamtime. They moved comfortably about the steep hills among tree ferns and beneath a towering canopy of Antarctic myrtle beech and mountain ash—the tallest flowering plants on earth. They drank the tannin-stained brown water from the creeks and ate a varied diet including ducks, eels and warrigal greens. They navigated their way down the steep cliffs to the coast, where they ate turban shells, abalone and mussels, leaving many middens strewn throughout the region as evidence of their feasts.

Latrobe's relationship with the Otways was entirely different. He struggled desperately to cut his way through the forest that twice repelled his advances. On his third sally, in March 1846, he commented on the seasonal vagaries of the Gellibrand River, writing that his party 'came to a dead halt, the whole valley being to our surprise, one wide lake'. Leaving the horses behind and partially stripping, carrying their kit above their heads, they forded the river and two days later became the first Europeans to reach Cape Otway.

It was one thing for Latrobe to reach the cape, but the fledgling colony now faced the huge challenge of finding a way to transport in men and materials to construct the lighthouse. After several failed attempts, William Roadknight eventually mapped a road, and George Smythe surveyed a sea approach, finding a landing place at the mouth of the Parker River. Through crashing surf, in tiny boats, the twenty-one polished reflectors and lamps of the lantern were landed, and after two years, on 29 August 1848, the lamp was lit.

The first light keeper was dismissed for mismanagement and 'improper and ungentlemanly language', and was replaced by Henry Bayles Ford, whose watch lasted thirty years, from 1848 until 1878. His wife, Mary Anne, gave birth to seven children at the remote outpost. Assistant keeper William Evans and his wife, Catherine, lived at the cape for twenty-two years, during which they lost two children in the space of eighteen months. For 142 years, a triple flash winked uninterrupted every eighteen seconds; mariners about to 'thread the needle'—a nineteenth-century description of navigating a sailing ship through Bass Strait—could see it up to 26 nautical miles offshore. The light was finally decommissioned in January 1994, after serving as the longest continuously operating light on the Australian mainland, and was replaced by an automatic solar light. Today it is a short drive on bitumen from the Great Ocean Road to the cape, making it difficult to visualise how isolated the place once was. The old lighthouse still stands, a white column rising above the stunted, windblown scrub, a sentinel keeping watch over the hazy blue of Bass Strait.

Grilled prawns with piri piri (*Camãreo com piri piri*)

On his second voyage of 1493–96, Christopher Columbus brought chilli seeds back from the New World to the Iberian Peninsula. Portuguese traders then carried the seeds to their African colonies in Angola and Mozambique. Chillies soon spread across Africa. In the African language of Swahili, piri piri translates as 'pepper pepper'. At some stage, Portuguese traders brought small red chillies back from Africa to Portugal, where they have been known as piri piri ever since and have given their name to the wonderful piquant sauce—*molho de piri piri*—that marries so well with fish. This sauce or marinade is on offer throughout Portugal in cafes, restaurants and bars. You will need to make it a week or two in advance. If you would prefer to take some sting out of the sauce, roast the chillies uncovered in a low oven for 15 minutes, then slip off the skins and remove the seeds.

Piri piri
1 cup extra-virgin olive oil
6 small red chillies, finely chopped
½ tablespoon sweet paprika
1 garlic clove, crushed
2 teaspoons salt
½ teaspoon dried oregano

Prawns
2 garlic cloves
2 small red chillies
1 teaspoon sweet paprika
1 teaspoon dried oregano
½ cup extra-virgin olive oil
1 kg (2 lb 3 oz) green king prawns, shelled,
    heads removed, de-veined
salt
lemon wedges

Combine the ingredients for the piri piri in a jar and shake vigorously. Leave in the refrigerator for a week or two for the flavours to develop.

Pound the garlic, chillies, paprika and oregano to a paste in a mortar. Transfer to a bowl and add the oil and prawns and mix well. Marinate in the refrigerator for 4 hours.

Thread the prawns onto metal skewers (or bamboo skewers soaked in water) and grill on a barbecue for 5–6 minutes, until opaque. Turn halfway through and baste constantly with the leftover marinade.

Come and get it
Place the prawns on a plate, sprinkle with salt and serve with lemon wedges and the piri piri.

Filipino prawn and sweet potato ukoy with sawsawan vinegar sauce

Ukoy fritters are cooked all over the Philippines and are a popular snack. The technique is a tough one to master properly; the difficulty is in getting the deep-frying right, as the fritter, made from a runny batter, needs to cohere as it cooks. A little practice and you will get the knack. If you are worried, make the batter thicker. The vinegar dipping sauce cuts the oil beautifully.

Sawsawan

2 garlic cloves
1 teaspoon salt
½ teaspoon pepper
½ cup vinegar
2 tablespoons light soy sauce

Ukoy

250 g (9 oz) small green prawns, heads removed, shelled and de-veined
½ cup jasmine rice
1 cup plain (all-purpose) flour
¼ cup cornflour (cornstarch)
1 egg
1 teaspoon salt
½ teaspoon ground white pepper
1 cup grated sweet potato
5 spring onions (scallions), finely chopped
handful of bean sprouts
1 litre (2 pints) peanut oil

For the sawsawan, grind the garlic, salt and pepper in a mortar to form a smooth paste. Add the vinegar and soy sauce and transfer to a bowl.

For the ukoy, bring a saucepan of salted water to the boil and cook the prawns until pink (3–4 minutes). Drain and reserve the water.

Grind the rice to a flour in a mortar and mix with the plain flour and cornflour.

Whisk the egg until fluffy, then add 1 cup of the prawn cooking water. Add the flour mixture, salt and pepper and beat until smooth. The batter should be a thick pouring consistency; if needed, add a little more prawn water. Stir in the sweet potato and half of the spring onions.

Pour boiling water over the bean sprouts, then drain and add to the batter.

Heat the peanut oil in a wok to around 190°C (375°F). Take a ladle of the batter, sprinkle on some of the extra spring onions and add 2–3 prawns, then pour the contents of the ladle into the hot oil. Use a wire strainer to gently coax the batter together to form a cake. Cook in small batches until crisp, then drain on paper towel.

Come and get it
Serve the ukoy alongside the bowl of sawsawan.

FISH

Salmon poached in court bouillon

The rich flavour of Atlantic salmon is showcased when poached in court bouillon. Serve with steamed baby potatoes tossed with dill or a salad of bitter greens. For a twist, serve on wasabi mashed potatoes (page 115). With a pair of scissors, cut nori sheets the size of the fish, spoon the potato onto plates, place the nori squares on top and finish with the salmon.

4 Atlantic salmon cutlets or thick fillets
court bouillon (page 3)
½ bottle dry white wine

Place the salmon in a wide, deep pan and cover with the cold court bouillon and wine. Bring to a simmer (do not boil), cooking the salmon for approximately 12–15 minutes. Use the shorter time if you like your salmon pink in the middle.

Come and get it
Remove the salmon with a slotted spoon and serve on warm plates. Perhaps top with a tablespoon of arame salad (page 194).

Grilled sardines with lemon and rosemary

The humble sardine is very good for you. It's full of omega-3 and selenium, and they are also clean and sustainable. But better than that—they're delicious. This simple recipe takes moments to prepare and only a few minutes to cook.

1 kg (2 lb 3 oz) Australian sardines, scaled and gutted
½ cup extra-virgin olive oil
1 lemon, juiced
1 large rosemary sprig, leaves picked
flaky salt and cracked pepper
lemon wedges
boiled potatoes
roasted capsicum (bell pepper)

Heat the grill of a barbecue. Make a dressing by combining the olive oil, lemon juice, rosemary, salt and pepper. Brush the sardines with the dressing and grill for a few minutes, until just starting to brown, then brush with more dressing and turn. Grill until browned on the other side.

Come and get it
Place the sardines in a bowl and scatter with lemon wedges. Serve with boiled potatoes and roasted capsicum.

The Géographe and the Naturaliste

Those captains who have scientists, or who may someday have them aboard their ships, must, upon departure, take a good supply of patience.

Nicolas Baudin

Napoléon Bonaparte had a fascination for all things Australian. In 1800, two ships departed from France on what is now considered perhaps the most important eighteenth-century scientific expedition to Australia. Their mission was to complete the French cartographic survey of the coast of Australia and to conduct detailed scientific investigations thereupon. The ships' complement of over two hundred passengers included three botanists, five zoologists, two mineralogists, three artists, five gardeners, two astronomers, two geographers, five doctors and a pharmacist. On 19 October 1800, the flagship *Géographe* under the command of Post Captain Nicolas Baudin, and her consort the *Naturaliste* under Captain Jacques Félix Emmanuel Hamelin, sailed from the port of Le Havre, near the mouth of the Seine.

The Western Australian coast was sighted on 27 May 1801. The *Géographe* and the *Naturaliste* were pounded by fierce storms in Géographe Bay. Helmsman Thomas Vasse was swept overboard by a giant wave off Wonnerup Beach, near today's town of Busselton, and was presumed lost at sea. Curiously, a local myth suggests that in 1834 Aboriginals showed British settlers the grave of a white man who, they said, used to sit gazing out to sea. This man was most likely poor Vasse, condemned to live out his days in lonely isolation awaiting the return of a ship that would never come.

After a detour to Coupang, in Dutch Indonesia, Baudin and his scientists made exhaustive studies of the geography and natural history of Tasmania, as well as detailed anthropological studies of its Aboriginal inhabitants. Their ethnographic work illustrates the problem of cultural relativism, especially in their observations of Aboriginal sexuality, which reveal more about the European preoccupation with love and marriage than about the complex hierarchies within Aboriginal society. Nevertheless, the studies represent the most detailed European accounts of first contact in Australia.

The expedition continued up the coast to an anchorage at Maria Island, then crossed Bass Strait. The two ships became separated; Hamelin surveyed Westernport and then headed for Port Jackson, while Baudin sailed westward, charting the Victorian and South Australian coastline, bestowing French names on landmarks that unbeknown to him had already been surveyed by Lieutenant James Grant. Near Kangaroo Island, on 8 April 1802, he unexpectedly sighted the British ship *Investigator* under the command of Lieutenant Matthew Flinders, who was carrying out a circumnavigation of the continent. Flinders named the place Encounter Bay after their historic meeting.

After further exploration, with a crew racked with scurvy and dysentery and ever-diminishing supplies of drinking water, Baudin charted a course for Port Jackson. By the time they sighted the entrance to the port, only four sailors were capable of work. A sympathetic Governor Phillip King sent some of Flinders' crew to help sail the stricken ship into the harbour. Governor King quickly gave relief, further rationing the colony's already meagre food supplies to help the recuperation of the sailors.

After a five-month stay in Sydney, Hamelin sailed the *Naturaliste* back to France, taking with him invalids and others Baudin thought unfit to continue, as well as the natural-history collections made thus far. Baudin purchased from Governor King the *Casuarina*, a 30-ton locally built schooner, which he placed under the command of Louis de Freycinet, to accompany the *Géographe* for the remainder of the expedition. On 17 November 1802, Baudin sailed from Sydney Harbour for King Island in Bass Strait to continue his survey.

The *Casuarina* was sent to survey the Hunter Islands, and then joined the *Géographe* on a running survey of Kangaroo Island. The *Casuarina* was then given just twenty days to survey St Vincent and Spencer gulfs, before meeting up again 900 miles further west in King George Sound. They revisited Géographe Bay and Shark Bay and sailed up the north-west coast, all the while collecting specimens that proved erroneous William Dampier's claims of more than a hundred years previously that the coast was devoid of life. British maps did not supersede Baudin's survey of this coast for over twenty years.

Baudin's health was deteriorating. Early chest pains had developed to coughing up blood. He sailed to Coupang once more, to re-provision, before pressing on to complete the surveys laid down in his instructions: the rest of the north-west coast, the Gulf of Carpentaria and the southern coast of New Guinea. But he was too late in the season; the south-east monsoon now opposed him. In the middle of the Arafura Sea, hopelessly fighting against the wind, with food and water running short, the kangaroos seasick and the emus requiring force-feeding, Baudin at last brought his two ships about and charted a course for home. He took pleasure in surprising his companions: 'No one was expecting it, for throughout the whole voyage no one has ever known where I was going or what I intended to do. Several of those who spent the whole night on deck went frequently to consult the compass for fear they had not heard aright'.

Baudin reached Isle de France, but died six weeks later, on 16 September 1803, of tuberculosis. He was buried, according to Louis de Freycinet, 'with all the honours due to his rank in the navy'.

The *Casuarina* was abandoned at Isle de France, and her crew transferred to the *Géographe* for the journey home. Their arrival, on 25 March 1804, was virtually ignored. The expedition took back over a hundred thousand specimens, including 2542 zoological species, for the collections of the Muséum d'Histoire Naturelle in Paris, and provided live plants and animals for the gardens and menageries of the museum and of Malmaison, the summer palace of Napoléon's wife, Joséphine. Only in recent years has the expedition been recognised for its contribution to the science and history of Australia, which have always been dominated by the English conquest story. Not only were the British dismissive of Baudin's expedition, but the French were not keen to promote a voyage that brought them no glory. A scapegoat was found in the deceased Baudin, and, in the official narrative of the voyage, his name, incredibly, was not even mentioned.

Simple Thai curry of gemfish

6 garlic cloves, skin on
3 small red chillies
6 cm (2 ⅓ in) fresh turmeric
2 cm (¾ in) ginger
2 cm (¾ in) galangal
2 cups coconut milk
500 g (1 lb 2 oz) skinless, boneless gemfish fillets,
    cut into bite-sized pieces
2 tablespoons fish sauce
steamed rice
coriander (cilantro) leaves

Pound the garlic, chilli, turmeric, ginger and galangal to paste in a mortar, or use a food processor.

Heat the coconut milk in a saucepan until just below boiling. Add the paste and slowly simmer for 5 minutes. Add the fish and simmer until cooked through. Add the fish sauce.

Come and get it
Serve on top of steamed rice and garnish with coriander.

Cantonese steamed snapper

This magnificent dish showcases the delightful sweet flesh of snapper. It presents beautifully for a banquet and is easy to prepare. My Cantonese stepmother Siu Mai taught me the recipe. She also introduced me to eating the fish cheeks and eyes, which after initial revulsion, I discovered are the tastiest morsels. At most tables I sit at, there is happily no competition for the best bits!

1 large snapper (about 3 kg/6 lb 10 oz), scaled and gutted
3 cm (1 in) ginger, finely julienned
3 garlic cloves, finely julienned
⅓ cup light soy sauce
1 tablespoon sesame oil
3 spring onions (scallions), sliced into strips
steamed rice

Make shallow crosscuts in the skin of the snapper on both sides. Lay the fish in a deep tray or dish that will fit inside a bamboo steamer. Scatter with the ginger and garlic and pour over the soy sauce and sesame oil. Leave the fish in a cool place for 1 hour, spooning the marinade over it every 10 minutes.

Scatter the fish with the spring onions and place in a bamboo steamer set over a wok of boiling water. Steam for 15–30 minutes, until the thickest part of the flesh comes away easily when prised with a fork. Monitor the water levels as the fish cooks.

Come and get it
Transfer the fish to a serving platter and pour over the dish juices. Serve with steamed rice.

Swordfish poached in champagne and lime

⅓ cup extra-virgin olive oil
4 swordfish steaks
4 garlic cloves, finely chopped
2 shallots, finely chopped
¼ bottle dry brut sparkling wine (champagne)
1 lime, zested and juiced
1 kaffir lime leaf
1 tablespoon sugar
salt and pepper
coriander (cilantro) leaves

Heat the olive oil in a large heavy-based frying pan and brown the swordfish steaks on each side. Remove to a plate and add the garlic and shallots to the pan. Fry until just colouring, then return the swordfish and add the sparkling wine. Bring to a gentle simmer. Add the lime zest and juice, kaffir lime leaf, sugar, salt and pepper. Poach the fish for a few minutes until cooked through.

Remove the fish with a slotted spoon and keep warm for a couple of minutes under a tea towel. Raise the heat in the pan to reduce the poaching liquid by half.

Come and get it
Place the swordfish on plates and pour over the sauce. Garnish with coriander.

Barramundi with lemon and olive dressing

This is a no-nonsense quick meal; all you have to do is make the dressing 12 or more hours in advance. If your barramundi is wild and fresh, the dish will be sublime. When I'm in the tropics, this is the perfect reward for a day's fishing—without the work of preparing a complex meal.

1 cup extra-virgin olive oil
2 lemons, zested
salt and pepper
4 plate-sized barramundi, scaled and gutted
1 cup kalamata olives, pitted

Combine the oil and lemon zest and add salt and pepper to taste. Allow the flavours to develop for 12 or more hours.

Heat the oven to 200°C (400°F). Smear the fish with some of the oil. Heat a little more of the oil in a very hot frying pan and sear each fish for 2 minutes on each side, then place on a tray with the olives and remaining oil. Bake in the oven for 5 minutes. The skin should be crispy and the flesh soft.

Come and get it
Serve with your favourite salad or on a bed of mashed potato.

Teriyaki yellowtail kingfish

Yellowtail kingfish is a great fighting fish. Its flesh has a strong, rich quality, but when cooked is surprisingly subtle. It is ideal for the teriyaki treatment. Teriyaki is a combination of two Japanese words: *teri* meaning lustre and shine, and *yaki* meaning grill. It is the mirin and sugar that bring out the lustre, while soy sauce gives colour. This is a simple dish to prepare with a magnificent result.

4 thick yellowtail kingfish cutlets
1 tablespoon soy sauce
1 tablespoon mirin
1 teaspoon sugar
extra-virgin olive oil
wakame salad (page 196)

Marinate the kingfish in the soy sauce, mirin and sugar for at least 1 hour, or up to overnight in the refrigerator.

Heat the grill of a barbecue and brush it with olive oil. Grill the kingfish until brown on one side, then pour over any leftover marinade and turn the fish to cook it on the other side.

Come and get it
Serve with wakame salad.

Serves 4

The Theft of the Ferret

By the 1880s, the days of piracy on the high seas were long over, so when the *Ferret* was stolen, the sensational news flashed around the world. On 25 June 1881, the *New York Times* ran an article 'A Steamer Stolen: How a Glasgow Firm Was Swindled'. The story of the elaborate ruse is as delightful as it is incredible.

In October 1880, inquiries were made to the Highland Railway Company of Scotland by Henderson and Company—supposedly a London firm of shipbrokers—stating that they were acting as agents for a Mr Smith, a very wealthy gentleman who was desirous of chartering a vessel to take his ailing wife on a cruise to the Mediterranean. Their first stop would be the port of Marseilles, to take on wealthy guests. References were checked and seemed to be in order, so a contract was signed for the first three months' charter of the *Ferret* and an amount of £270 was paid.

Shortly afterwards, a William Wallace presented himself at one of Glasgow's leading ship-store merchants claiming he was purser of the *Ferret* and was acting as an agent for Mr Smith, a close relative of the First Lord of the Admiralty, who desired to favour the firm with the contract of provisioning the vessel. No expense was spared. The provisions for six months included silver plate and cutlery, fine china and crystal, and a large stock of the highest class of wine from London. A bill for £1490 was presented, for which Wallace gave a certified draft of the amount, payable in three months. Checks were made with the bank in London and the funds were available.

The *Ferret* steamed from Clyde to Cardiff crewed by runners. She coaled up and a new crew was shipped, and after waiting out storms in Milford Haven for a week she sailed for Marseilles. On 11 November she was reported passing Gibraltar. After that, nothing more was heard of her. After three months, the Highland Railway Company applied for a renewal of the charter money, but there was none. Further inquiries showed that Henderson and Company didn't exist; nor did the wealthy Mr Smith. When the stevedores in Glasgow presented their bill at the bank, they learnt that the money had been withdrawn and no funds were available. A watch was organised at every port at which the *Ferret* might put in, but there was no trace. She had been stolen, and, worse yet, there were stories of wreckage washing up on the Spanish coast.

Meanwhile, somewhere in the mid Atlantic, in between bottles of London's finest, the crew was busy changing the *Ferret*'s livery to the *Benton*. Evidently, the *Ferret* had stolen back past Gibraltar under cover of darkness and snuck out into the wide Atlantic Ocean, and articles belonging to the ship—a lifeboat and buoys—had been tossed overboard to make it appear that she had sunk. She crossed the Atlantic to Santos, in Brazil. Using forged documents, she took on £8000-worth of coffee to return to Marseilles, but as soon as she was out of sight of land she set a course for Cape Town. Once again the livery was changed, and the *Benton* became the *India*. Her cargo was sold for £13 000, and she took on a new skipper, Robert Holmes Wright. When an attempt to sell the ship fell through, she hastily departed port and was soon enveloped in the vastness of the Southern Indian Ocean.

The *India* sailed for Port Phillip. On 20 April 1881, Constable McKenzie, who was monitoring the shipping at Port Phillip Heads, recognised the ship from a description, and realised that the *India* could well be the missing *Ferret*. He notified the commissioner of customs, who, with 'exemplary promptitude', dispatched a telegram to the customs department at Williamstown.

The *India* dropped anchor in Hobson's Bay, and Mr Smith and his wife alighted. Attempts were immediately made to sell the ship. Smith wanted £10 000 but he was offered only £8500. The port authorities' suspicions were further raised by the fires on board that were kept alight even though she was in port, suggesting the possibility of her needing to get steam up at short notice. Also, none of the crew had come ashore.

On 27 April, at 9 a.m., customs officers and police boarded the vessel. A slight examination afforded ample evidence she was indeed the *Ferret*: the name had been filed off the ship's bell and removed from the records. Smith had absconded, leaving his wife in Melbourne. According to the *Williamstown Chronicle* on 30 April 1881, 'When our reporter went on board ... the crew appeared in a muddled state from liquor. The Captain was in his cabin, not to be seen; and the chief officer, on being questioned gave a rambling statement, out of which but little could be made'. The crew obviously knew the game was up and were hard at work finishing off as much of the expensive London plonk as they could put down.

Warrants were issued for the arrest of the master, Smith and Wallace. Smith was arrested in Seymour; the master was eventually arrested for drunkenness and assault. At the subsequent court hearings the whole story came to light. Smith was actually James Stuart Henderson, a notorious swindler known to the English police. William Wallace's real name was Joseph John Walker, and the master was Edward Rashleigh Carylon. At the trial no account was taken of the series of frauds in foreign ports; nor were they found guilty of the theft of the *Ferret*. They were, however, convicted of conspiracy to defraud the intended purchasers of the vessel in Melbourne, and of conspiracy to deceive the customs and trade commissioner by changing the name of the ship. Henderson and Walker were sentenced to seven years in Melbourne's Pentridge Jail, and Carylon to three and a half.

The Highland Railway authorised their Melbourne agent to sell the *Ferret*, and she passed to the Adelaide Steamship Company. In 1904 the Norwegian vessel *Ethel* wrecked on the southern Yorke Peninsula in bad weather. The *Ferret* came to her aid but could not help and steamed to Troubridge Island to raise the alarm. Incredibly, sixteen years later the *Ferret* ran aground and was wrecked on the same beach. The crew managed to get to shore but her cargo of Christmas grog never reached its final destination—the workers at the nearby gypsum mines at Inneston saw to that.

Turkish baked bonito

This rustic eastern-Mediterranean dish is known in Turkey as *firinda palamut* and is an excellent way of preparing the strongly flavoured bonito. Carrot and celery can be added to give the dish more body.

1 medium bonito (about 2 kg/4 lb 6 oz), gutted
flaky salt
2 tomatoes, peeled and sliced
1 onion, sliced in thin rings
3 long green chillies, halved lengthwise and seeded
¼ bunch flat-leaf parsley, roughly chopped
2 bay leaves
1 lemon, peeled and sliced
½ cup extra-virgin olive oil
fresh pide

Cut the bonito crosswise into cutlets 2 cm (¾ in) thick. Pat them dry with paper towel and place in a baking dish. Sprinkle with a little salt.

Preheat the oven to 180°C (350°F). Lay the tomato, onion, chilli and parsley over the fish. Add the bay leaves and lemon and pour on the oil. Add enough water to cover the base of the dish and prevent the fish from sticking. Cover with foil and bake until the chillies are tender (around 30 minutes). Remove the foil and bake until the fish browns slightly.

Come and get it
Place the cutlets on plates and spoon over the sauce. Serve with pide.

Serves 4

Crispy snapper with tomato kecap

1 litre (2 pints) peanut oil
2 garlic cloves, sliced
3 shallots, sliced
2 cm (¾ in) ginger, finely sliced
1 small red chilli (or more to taste), sliced
2 tomatoes, chopped
2 tablespoons fish sauce
¼ cup kecap manis (sweet soy sauce)
2 lemons, juiced
½ bunch coriander (cilantro), chopped, plus extra leaves
    to garnish
1 large butchered snapper fillet (skin and wing on)
plain (all-purpose) flour

Heat a heavy-based saucepan and add a small splash of the oil. Fry the garlic, shallots, ginger and chilli until just brown. Add the tomatoes and cook until just softening. Add the fish sauce, kecap manis and lemon juice and stir well. Remove from the heat and stir in the coriander.

Heat the remaining oil in a wok to 180°C (350°F). Roll the fish in flour and deep-fry until golden brown. Drain on paper towel.

Come and get it
Place the fish on a serving platter and pour over the tomato sauce. Garnish with coriander and serve immediately.

Deep-fried turmeric sardines with lime and chilli dip

This dish is the essence of simplicity and will work well with any oily fish, but I like it best with sardines. Their bones become crumbly when deep-fried and are edible.

Dip
2 limes, juiced
2 tablespoons fish sauce
1 tablespoon sugar
3 small red chillies, finely sliced
handful of coriander (cilantro) leaves

Sardines
12 Australian sardines, scaled and gutted
¼ cup salt
3 cups peanut oil
¼ cup turmeric
coriander (cilantro) leaves

Mix the dip ingredients in a bowl and set aside.

Marinate the sardines in the salt for 5 minutes. Heat the oil in a wok to 180°C (350°F). Rinse the salt from the sardines and pat dry. Dust with turmeric and deep-fry until crisp. Drain on paper towel.

Come and get it
Serve the sardines on a platter with the dip alongside. Scatter with coriander leaves.

King George whiting with lemon, capers and parsley

The French scientist Georges Cuvier named King George whiting after King George Sound in Western Australia, which was where the first described specimen was taken. It is pretty hard to beat King George whiting simply dusted in flour and pan-fried in a little butter. The sweet, delicate flavour is superb. This simple recipe includes just a few extra ingredients.

4 King George whiting fillets
plain (all-purpose) flour
salt and pepper
120 g (4 oz) unsalted butter
1 tablespoon small salted capers, soaked in water for a few
    minutes then rinsed well
1 lemon, juiced, plus extra slices to garnish
½ cup dry white wine
handful of flat-leaf parsley sprigs, finely chopped

Roll the whiting in flour seasoned with salt and pepper.

Heat the butter in a heavy-based frying pan and add the whiting. Fry gently until golden brown on the first side, then turn. Add the capers and lemon juice. Remove the whiting to warm serving plates when just cooked through. Raise the heat of the pan, pour in the wine and boil for a few seconds.

Come and get it

Pour the sauce over the fish and sprinkle with flaky salt and cracked pepper. Garnish with lemon slices and parsley.

Ceviche of sweep

Ceviche, a simple and refreshing dish of raw fish soaked in citrus juice, is popular in various forms through Latin America. The acid in the juice causes the protein in the fish to denature, effectively cooking it without heat. It is critical that the fish is very fresh, preferably just caught. In Peru it is served with sweet potato or boiled corn, in Mexico with corn chips, and in Ecuador with popcorn or nuts. I think it makes a fantastic starter on its own.

1 kg (2 lb 3 oz) sweep fillets (or fillets of other firm white fish
   such as snapper or blue-eye trevalla), skinless
200 ml (7 fl oz) lemon juice
200 ml (7 fl oz) blood orange or lime juice
1 garlic clove, crushed
1 small red chilli, finely chopped
1 red onion, finely sliced
1 tomato, finely diced
2 tablespoons chopped flat-leaf parsley
2 tablespoons chopped coriander (cilantro)
flaky salt and cracked pepper

Cut the fish into 1 cm (⅓ in) cubes and place in a bowl. Pour the citrus juices over the top and leave to marinate for an hour or so, or up to 3 hours if you prefer. The fish will have turned opaque.

Come and get it
Add the remaining ingredients just before serving and season to taste.

Mesopotamian carp

Scurrilous rumours and innuendo abound about carp. To set the matter straight, they are not all bones; in fact, 40 per cent of the fillet contains none at all, and the flavour is delicious. However, it is important to remove the skin as soon as possible as there is a layer of fat between the meat and skin that can make the fish taste muddy. Variations of this dish are popular along the Tigris and Euphrates rivers, the cradle of civilisation, where carp are plentiful. A famous dish from Iraq is *mazgouf*, where carp is cut lengthwise and opened, salted and propped on wooden sticks beside an open fire of pomegranate wood. After 45 minutes, the fish is placed directly on top of the hot embers to finish the cooking, and then it is served with salad and flatbread.

Fresh turmeric is used in this dish, a tropical rhizome that looks like a small knob of ginger. Use dried turmeric if unavailable. The recipe also uses ground dried lime, available from Middle Eastern stores—or you can dry lime skins yourself (in a warm place such as on top of a heater) and then grind them in a mortar or food processor.

2 x 3 kg (6 lb 10 oz) whole carp, scaled and gutted
1 large onion, chopped
3 large tomatoes, peeled and chopped
2–3 cm (1 in) fresh turmeric, finely chopped
1 tablespoon ground dried lime
salt and pepper
extra-virgin olive oil
steamed rice

Remove the skin from the carp with a sharp knife, peeling it off in strips.

Preheat the oven to 180°C (350°F). Put the onion, tomatoes, turmeric, dried lime and salt and pepper in a food processor and blend to a paste. Place the carp in a large baking dish and coat with the mixture inside and out. Drizzle some olive oil over the top. Bake for 30 minutes or until cooked through.

Come and get it
Cut the fish in portions and serve on rice with the cooking juices spooned over the top.

Indonesian snapper

¼ cup peanut oil
4 snapper fillets, skin on
1 onion, chopped
6 garlic cloves, crushed
small red chillies to taste, finely chopped
2 cm (¾ in) galangal, finely chopped
1 kaffir lime leaf
½ cup coconut milk
2 cups fish stock (page 2)
½ cup kecap manis (sweet soy sauce)
steamed rice

Heat two-thirds of the oil in a heavy-based frying pan over medium heat and fry the snapper pieces for 2 minutes on each side. Transfer to a plate and keep warm under a tea towel.

Add the remaining oil to the pan and fry the onion, garlic, chilli, galangal and kaffir lime and cook until the onion is starting to soften. Add the coconut milk, fish stock and kecap manis and raise the heat. Reduce the sauce by half.

Add the snapper, turn down the heat and simmer for 10 minutes.

Come and get it
Place the snapper on plates and spoon the sauce over the top. Serve with steamed rice.

Greek baked eel

The eel is much maligned in Australia, largely because of its resemblance to the snake. Eels make wonderful eating and are plentiful in the estuaries and creeks of south-eastern Australia. They were much favoured by Aboriginal people. The golden rule for filleting eel is a sharp knife, as they are slippery things. Some people like to use a nail to anchor the eel through the head to the workbench. Insert your filleting knife behind the head and run the knife down to the backbone; cut off one fillet. Turn the eel over and repeat the process. Then, trim off the rib bones and stomach lining as you would any fish and cut into portions.

This recipe uses the Greek wine mavrodafni, a fortified variety almost black in colour that hails from the Achaia region in the northern Peloponnese. It is the preferred wine for Holy Communion in the Greek Orthodox Church. If you can't get your hands on a bottle, use a bold port such as one from Rutherglen in Victoria.

1 kg (2 lb 3 oz) eel fillets
¼ cup plain (all-purpose) flour
½ cup extra-virgin olive oil
4 onions, chopped
2 garlic cloves
4 tomatoes, roughly chopped
1 tablespoon dried Greek oregano (rigani)
1 cup mavrodafni or port
salt
handful of flat-leaf parsley sprigs, roughly chopped
cracked pepper
crusty bread

Roll the eel fillets in the flour. Heat the oil in a large ovenproof frying pan and fry the fillets until lightly brown. Drain on paper towel.

Add the onions and garlic to the pan and fry until soft. Add the tomatoes, oregano, mavrodafni or port and salt and cook for a further 10 minutes or so, until the tomatoes are soft.

Preheat the oven to 180°C (350°F). Return the eel to the pan, bury it in the sauce, and transfer to the oven. Bake for 30–45 minutes.

Come and get it
Scoop the eel into bowls and spoon over the sauce. Sprinkle with parsley and cracked pepper and serve with crusty bread.

Tanzanian fish masala

The east coast of Africa is no stranger to spice. Zanzibar, the island off the coast of Tanzania, was once a centre of the spice trade. Nutmeg, cinnamon and pepper were produced there, and at one stage it was the world's leading supplier of cloves. This dish reflects the influence of the Arab traders and the spices that crossed the Indian Ocean with them.

500 g (1 lb 2 oz) fresh or tinned roma tomatoes
small red chillies to taste
6 garlic cloves
⅓ cup mustard oil
1 tablespoon cumin seeds
1 tablespoon ajowan or caraway seeds
¼ cup tomato paste
¼–½ cup lime juice
2 tablespoons garam masala
1 teaspoon ground cumin
½ teaspoon turmeric
salt
handful of coriander (cilantro) sprigs, chopped,
    plus extra to garnish
4 perch fillets or other firm white fish fillets, skinless
steamed rice

Combine the tomatoes, chillies and garlic in a food processor and purée.

Heat the mustard oil in a frying pan until very hot and add the cumin and ajowan (or caraway) seeds and stir until bubbly. Add the tomato, chilli and garlic purée and cook for 5 minutes. Add the tomato paste, lime juice, garam masala, ground cumin, turmeric and salt and simmer until thick. Remove from the heat and allow to cool to room temperature. When cool, add the coriander.

Preheat the oven to 180°C (350°F). Place the fish fillets on a non-stick baking tray and spread the sauce over the top. Bake for 10–15 minutes.

Come and get it
Serve on rice and garnish with extra coriander.

Rockling in fragrant coconut

This is a very quick and easy Asian-inspired dish. The hint of aniseed in the Thai basil complements the kaffir lime and lemongrass. If you like, add bean sprouts and snow peas in the last minute of cooking.

1 lemongrass stalk, white part only, roughly chopped
2 garlic cloves, skin on
small green chillies to taste
2 tablespoons peanut oil
1 cup coconut milk
500 g (1 lb 2 oz) rockling, cut into bite-sized pieces
3 kaffir lime leaves, finely sliced
15 Thai basil leaves, plus extra to garnish
fish sauce to taste
½ teaspoon salt
steamed rice
coriander (cilantro) leaves

Pound the lemongrass, garlic and chillies to a paste in a mortar, or use a food processor.

Heat the peanut oil in a wok and fry the paste for around 3 minutes. Add the coconut milk and heat to almost boiling, then add the fish and simmer until cooked through. Add the kaffir lime leaves, basil and fish sauce.

Come and get it
Spoon over hot rice and garnish with extra Thai basil leaves and coriander leaves.

Steamed nannygai with lime

I love steaming whole fish; the flesh becomes very succulent. If you can't get nannygai, use snapper.

1 nannygai weighing around 800 g (1 lb 12 oz), scaled and gutted
2 limes, 1 zested and juiced and 1 finely sliced
3 garlic cloves, finely chopped
4 spring onions (scallions), 2 finely chopped and 2 sliced into
   2.5 cm (1 in) lengths
1 tablespoon fish sauce
1 tablespoon Chinese rice wine
1 teaspoon sugar
1 kaffir lime leaf, finely sliced
coriander (cilantro) leaves
steamed rice

Cut three diagonal slits in each side of the nannygai. Rub the cavity of the fish with the lime zest, garlic and finely chopped spring onion. Lay the fish in a deep tray or dish that will fit inside a bamboo steamer.

Combine the lime juice, fish sauce, rice wine and sugar and pour it over the fish. Lay the lime slices, lengths of spring onion and kaffir lime strips on top. Place in a bamboo steamer set over a wok of boiling water and steam for 10–15 minutes, until the thickest part of the flesh comes away easily when prised with a fork.

Come and get it
Transfer the fish to a serving platter, pour over the dish juices and garnish with coriander. Serve with steamed rice.

Firestorm at Cape Naturaliste

Several ships have been lost off Cape Naturaliste, where there are dangerous reefs and forceful currents. On 8 July 1840, American whalers the *Samuel Wright*, the *North America* and the *Governor Endicott* were wrecked in a gale. In 1844, the *Halycon* was completely destroyed, and the *Day Dawn*, the *Gaff* and the *Dao* were blown ashore in gales. In 1895, the Danish ship *Phoenix*, heavy with her cargo of jarrah, was also blown ashore, as was the *Paragon*.

In response to the plethora of maritime disasters, a lighthouse was constructed atop the 300-feet-high bluff at Cape Naturaliste. The lens and turntable weighed a gargantuan 12.5 tons and were hauled in from nearby Eagle Bay on bullock wagons. The incandescent vapourised kerosene lamp was first lit in 1904. Patrick Baird was appointed the first lightkeeper. On 31 January 1907, some 800 nautical miles south-west of Cape Leeuwin, the *Carnarvon Castle* caught fire and sank, and the crew abandoned ship into two lifeboats. At the mercy of the Southern Indian Ocean, they bobbed across the sea, eventually landing at Cape Naturaliste, where they were cared for by the lightkeeper and his family until they were well enough to travel. Two sailors had died at sea and one died two days after coming ashore.

After the shipwrecked survivors departed, life returned to normal at Cape Naturaliste. The summer storms moved to the autumn calms, followed by the cold winds of winter and a succession of storms off the Indian Ocean. Then in July, during an horrendous storm, the light station was hit by a fireball. Ethel Bovell, daughter of the lightkeeper, recorded the event:

Father was the only one on duty, the time was 9.00 am. One of the Assistant Lightkeepers had gone 25 miles to the small town of Busselton for supplies and food for the three families. The second Assistant had gone to Yallingup Cave House to collect all the postal mail, papers etc. for the lighthouse which was collected once a week.

It was 8.30 am, a storm had been raging for 5 days, then it turned into a severe electric storm with terrible flashes of lightning and thunder which was deafening, then everything went quiet all of a sudden. We were standing looking out of the window facing North East, wondering if we could now go outside. It became very dark, then a large red ball of fire slowly appeared on the horizon. We watched it as it slowly moved towards us, the air became very warm. We were frightened and then as it became closer, Mother quickly pushed we children under the beds. She got under a heavy dining table, only just in time as the fire ball hit our house, breaking windows, the telephone rang violently, then burst from the wall with a loud explosion, the noise terrible. Mother became worried as Father was on duty up at the lighthouse. She put a coat on and rushed out leaving us screaming under the beds, to see if Father was safe. The pathway was all ripped up, to a depth of approximately 4 feet along the underground phone line from our house to the lighthouse. The wind was so strong it almost knocked Mother over.

When she reached the lighthouse and went upstairs, on the first landing things were in a mess. Father said later he put his hand on the phone to put through a weather report, and it blew up and out from the wall knocking my Father unconscious. A long large cupboard, which was strongly

bolted with long bolts to the wall, was blown from the wall. It had a lightning conductor running up the wall behind the cupboard from the ground to the top of the lighthouse dome and outside. This was twisted and torn. Everything was tossed and smashed up, that had been in the path of the fire ball. It was terrible.

After the fire ball struck, there was loud thunder and lightning, like hell let loose for about an hour. Then the severity of the storm subsided and it became very quiet. Very heavy rain came down and lasted for a few hours, slowly stopping. Then everything cleared, the sun shone through and it looked so peaceful with raindrops glistening on trees and flowers.

The absence of the two keepers placed a heavy burden on Mother. We two children were her only helpers at the time, so she sent us two miles to ask the farmer, Mr Curtis, for help. He had to ride horseback twelve miles to Caves House, Yallingup, to the nearest phone, for help from Busselton.

A doctor had to be brought 25 miles to the lighthouse. We were cut off with no 'phones. Father was ill and had a long cut on his head which had to be sutured up. Mother was also suffering from shock. Father was ill for eight weeks and off duty.

It is surprising the amount of damage a fire ball causes when it strike its terror and I never want to see another one. It left us all in a highly nervous condition for some time and every time there was a bad storm we were all terrified as to what would happen next. In the years to follow, we had many severe storms in the winter, but we never saw another fire ball, which seems to be something that rarely happens.

It takes years to overcome the fear of storms.

Tunisian-style flathead with harissa and olives

8 flathead tails
½ cup plain (all-purpose) flour
salt and pepper
½ cup extra-virgin olive oil
1 onion, finely chopped
2 garlic cloves, finely chopped
1 tablespoon harissa (page 186)
500 g (1 lb 2 oz) tomatoes, peeled, seeded and chopped
1 cinnamon stick
1 cup kalamata olives, pitted
1 tablespoon lemon juice
steamed couscous
chopped flat-leaf parsley

Roll the flathead tails in flour seasoned with salt and pepper. Heat half of the oil in a large, heavy-based frying pan and fry the flathead until golden. Transfer to a plate and keep warm under a tea towel.

Add the remaining oil to the pan and fry the onion and garlic until the onion is translucent. Stir in the harissa then add the tomatoes and cinnamon and cook until thickened. Stir in the olives. Add the fish, bury it in the sauce and simmer gently for 5 minutes. Add the lemon juice.

Come and get it
Serve the fish and sauce on a bed of couscous and sprinkle with parsley.

Serves 4

Baked coconut masala pomfret

1 coconut
4 small silver pomfret, about 15 cm (6 in) and 300–400 g (10 ½–14 oz)
    each, scaled and gutted
1 teaspoon flaky salt
½ teaspoon freshly ground black pepper
½ teaspoon chilli powder
½ teaspoon turmeric
2 small green chillies, roughly chopped
5 cm (2 in) ginger, roughly chopped
8 garlic cloves
1 cup coriander (cilantro) leaves, plus extra to garnish
1 teaspoon ground cumin
2 teaspoons ground coriander
1 lime, juiced
1 teaspoon brown sugar
foil or banana leaves
steamed rice

Crack open the coconut with a chisel and reserve the sweet water inside (drink it or use it in another dish). Remove the shell, then take off the brown skin attached to the flesh with a paring knife. Finely grate the flesh of half the coconut and leave the rest for another use.

Fillet the fish, leaving the skin on.

Combine the salt, pepper, chilli powder and turmeric. Lay the fillets skin-side down and rub the mixture into the flesh.

Place the coconut and remaining ingredients in a food processor and blend to a paste.

Lay a fish fillet in the centre of a piece of foil or banana leaf and spread with a generous amount of paste. Top with another fillet skin-side up and wrap into a neat parcel. Repeat with the remaining fish and paste.

If using foil, heat the oven to 200°C (400°F) and cook the fish on a tray for 15–20 minutes, until the flesh is opaque and flakes when prised with a fork.

If using banana leaves, place the parcels in a bamboo steamer set over a wok of boiling water and steam for around 30 minutes.

Come and get it
Open the parcels and gently lift the fish onto a bed of rice. Pour over any juices in the parcels and garnish with coriander.

Serves 4

Barbecued sambal stingray

This dish is quintessential hawker food from Malaysia and Singapore. I have suggested to serve it with cincaluk, which is a bottled sauce made from tiny shrimp that have been left to rot in the sun with rice until the mixture turns pinky brown. It smells like cheesy rotten fish, but is so delicious, especially with this stingray! Peranakans (a group with Chinese and Malay heritage) put it on everything. You can find it in Asian stores.

1 tablespoon tamarind pulp
¼ cup hot water
8 shallots
4 garlic cloves
1 tablespoon shrimp paste
2 tablespoons dried red chillies
2 slices of galangal
⅓ cup peanut oil
2 tablespoons coconut cream
salt
4 x 250 g (9 oz) skinned stingray (skate) wings
banana leaves or foil
sliced shallots
coriander (cilantro) leaves
lime wedges
cincaluk

Combine the tamarind pulp and hot water, stirring to break up and dissolve the tamarind. Leave for 5 minutes, then strain out the solids.

Smash the shallots in their skins with the back of a cleaver or in a mortar. Place in a food processor with the garlic, shrimp paste, chillies and galangal and blend to a paste. Add a little water if necessary.

Heat the oil in a wok and fry the paste over medium heat until fragrant. Stir in the tamarind water, then turn the heat down to a simmer and add the coconut cream. Stir until a thick paste consistency is reached. Remove from the heat, season with salt and allow to cool.

Run a knife along the wings to remove the tough cartilage from the flesh. Lay the stingray wings on banana leaves or sheets of foil and coat with the paste on both sides. Roll the parcels up. Grill on the barbecue for around 10 minutes, turning once, until the stingray is cooked through.

Come and get it
Unwrap the parcels and lift the stingray onto plates. Pour any cooking juices over the top and serve with sliced shallots, coriander leaves, lime and cincaluk.

North African bonito with tomato, chickpeas and preserved lemon

pinch of saffron threads
¼ cup extra-virgin olive oil
3 garlic cloves, crushed
3 cm (1 in) ginger, finely chopped
3 teaspoons ground coriander
400 g (14 oz) tinned tomatoes
500 g (1 lb 2 oz) cooked chickpeas (or tinned
    chickpeas, rinsed)
1 preserved lemon, skin only, rinsed and finely sliced
750 g (1 lb 10 oz) skinless, boneless bonito fillets,
    diced into bite-sized pieces
salt and pepper
½ cup roughly chopped flat-leaf parsley
⅓ cup roughly chopped coriander (cilantro)
steamed couscous
extra flat-leaf parsley and coriander (cilantro) leaves

Soak the saffron in a little warm water.

Heat a large heavy-based saucepan over medium heat and add the oil, garlic and ginger and cook until the garlic just starts to colour. Stir in the ground coriander. Add the tomatoes, chickpeas, preserved lemon, saffron (and its water) and ½ cup of water and cook for 15 minutes.

Add the bonito and carefully stir through. Season with salt and pepper to taste. Reduce the heat and simmer for 5 minutes, until the fish is cooked through. Stir in the parsley and coriander.

Come and get it
Serve the stew on a bed of couscous garnished with extra parsley and coriander.

Serves 4

Tahitian rock-cod salad

Ceviche is a well-known dish of marinated raw fish (page 74); numus is another version but less known. (I first tasted numus on Melville Island north of Darwin—it is popular on Australia's north coast and in the Torres Strait, as well as Papua New Guinea and parts of the Pacific.) This salad is neither ceviche nor numus as the lime doesn't cook through the fish so the inside remains raw. It's a great luncheon dish on a hot summer's day when you've just come back with a boatload of fresh fish. A grass skirt and a coconut-shell brassiere are entirely optional.

1 kg (2 lb 3 oz) rock-cod fillets (or other firm white fish), skinless
1 tablespoon flaky salt
1 coconut
1 cup lime juice
1 red onion, finely sliced in rings
3 tomatoes, quartered
1 cucumber, finely sliced
1 red capsicum (bell pepper), sliced in chunky strips
4 spring onions (scallions), finely sliced on the diagonal
lime wedges
coriander (cilantro) sprigs

Cut the fish into bite-sized chunks and toss in a bowl with the salt. Leave to marinate in the refrigerator for a couple of hours.

Crack open the coconut with a chisel and reserve the sweet water inside. Remove the shell, then take off the brown skin attached to the flesh with a paring knife. Finely grate the flesh.

Rinse the salt from the fish under cold water and gently dry the fish with a clean tea towel.

Combine the coconut water and flesh, lime juice, red onion, tomato, cucumber, capsicum and spring onion in a bowl. Gently toss through the fish and chill until ready to serve.

Come and get it
Garnish with lime wedges and lots of coriander.

Commander, Governor, Pirate, Admiral

In his long career, William Bligh survived two mutinies. The first was the *Bounty* mutiny in 1789, and the second was the Rum Rebellion, when he was Governor of New South Wales.

Bligh stepped ashore at Sydney on 8 August 1806 to succeed the ailing Philip Gidley King as governor of the Colony of New South Wales. He had left his wife, Elizabeth, in London, and was accompanied by his daughter Mary and her husband, Lieutenant Charles Putland.

Sydney was a drunken society. Rum was its tipple, and the New South Wales Corps controlled its distribution. Bligh saw rum as an instrument of debilitation that helped the corps maintain its power; he railed against the consumption of the drink. The colony was on the verge of starvation, partly due to the Hawkesbury Floods, partly because of decreased supplies arriving by ship due to the war with France, and also because of the monopolistic trading of the corps and its abuse of convict labour. Bligh organised flood relief and promised the settlers that the government stores would buy their produce after the next harvest. But his bad language, violent temper and pedantic adherence to rules and regulations inhibited his effectiveness to command. All of this brought him on a collision course with the New South Wales Corps and its entrepreneurial leader John Macarthur, whom after a violent quarrel Bligh had clasped in irons and thrown into jail.

From his cell, Macarthur engineered a coup. He had his second in command, Major George Johnston, assume the title of lieutenant governor, claiming that 'insurrection and massacre' were imminent and that Bligh was planning 'to subvert the laws of the country' and 'to terrify and influence the Courts of justice'. Before Bligh could rally support from the colonists and the nearest garrison, on the Hawkesbury, the corps—under the command of Johnston—in full band and colours marched on Government House. After a brief standoff with Bligh's feisty daughter, who held them off with a parasol, they arrested the governor.

Adamant that he alone held the king's authority to govern, Bligh remained in confinement in Sydney for more than twelve months. He refused to travel to England, and refused passage on any boat that wasn't a naval vessel. Eventually, in February 1809, he relented, and agreed to sail with his recently widowed daughter on the *Porpoise*. A large crowd, including many of his supporters from Hawkesbury, gathered at the docks to farewell him. As the *Porpoise* weighed anchor, Bligh had the captain placed under arrest and in a fit of rage ordered the ship's guns to be rolled out and trained on those on the docks, which included members of the New South Wales Corps, his jailers and tormentors. Bligh was eventually persuaded against firing, and the *Porpoise* sailed for Van Diemen's Land. Bligh hoped to curry the favour there of Governor Collins.

On his arrival in Hobart, Bligh was cheered as captain-general and governor in chief of the Colony of New South Wales. Collins vacated Government House so that Bligh and Mary could take up residence. Bligh described the premises as 'a poor miserable shell of three rooms with the walls a brick thick, neither wind or waterproof and without conveniences'.

Collins quickly grew tired of Bligh, who incessantly interfered and meddled in local affairs. Bligh placarded the parade ground with notices saying that all who felt aggrieved were to go to him for redress, and in response Collins withdrew the guard on Government House. In a fit of pique, Bligh returned to the *Porpoise*. A few weeks later, in another rage, Bligh had the governor's son tied up and flogged with two dozen lashes for 'insubordination'.

Collins found Bligh's behaviour 'unhandsome in several respects' and decreed that anyone victualling or associating with the *Porpoise* would be dealt with as 'abettors of sedition and enemies of the peace and prosperity of the colony'. To survive, Bligh resorted to piracy. For the following six months he plundered the maritime commerce of the Derwent. Incoming ships were apprehended, boarded and their supplies commandeered. It was only when Bligh heard from a passing whaler of the imminent arrival of Governor Macquarie in Sydney that he quit the Derwent and sailed the *Porpoise* back to the mainland.

Bligh arrived too late to hear Macquarie's decree on 1 January 1810 of 'my painful duty to be thus compelled to publicly announce His Majesty's high displeasure and disapprobation of the mutinous and outrageous conduct displayed in the forcible and unwarrantable removal of his late representative, William Bligh, and of the tumultuous proceedings connected therewith'. Macquarie's orders were to allow Bligh to return to Sydney to gather evidence for the court martial of Major George Johnston. Bligh's day in court was no great revenge: Johnston was merely cashiered from the regiment, and Macarthur, who had previously scurried back to London to put his own case to the powers that be, was restrained from returning to New South Wales by an instruction that if he did so he was to be arrested and tried for treason. Bligh eventually sailed for England on 12 May 1810 after being—in the words of Macquarie—a 'great plague'. He was promoted to rear-admiral of the Blue and later to vice-admiral.

Sushi

Sushi, with its foundations of vinegared rice and the freshest raw fish, can be a work of art with innumerable variations. But it can also be very easy to prepare, at least a simple version of it. Sushi is naturally healthy food, although there are plenty of ways to make it even more so and to change the flavour. You can use brown rice instead of white, and forego the sugar or substitute it with honey or rice malt. Tofu can be used to make vegetarian sushi. I think sushi at home is best removed from strict traditions and used as a platform for your own creativity.

The two types of sushi in this recipe are nigiri, which are fingers of rice topped with seafood, and nori-maki or 'California rolls'. These rolls are ideal for school lunches. When our kids were at primary school in the small rural town where we live, they were teased mercilessly by their ham-sandwich-gobbling classmates for eating sushi. In those days, no one had seen it, especially in the country. Now with sushi available in virtually every Australian shopping mall it should be no big deal.

Sushi rice

4 cups short-grain white rice
½ cup rice vinegar
1 tablespoon salt
½ cup sugar

Nigiri ideas

wasabi paste
thin slices of fresh raw fish (almost
    anything, although good
    varieties include tuna, whiting
    and snapper)
thin slices of green prawns (or
    cooked if you prefer)
thin slices of tofu
nori sheets cut in thin ribbons
raw beetroot cut in small diamonds

Nori-maki ideas

nori sheets
lengths of spring onion
tinned tuna
strips of raw beetroot
thin strips of raw fish
thin strips of tofu

Wash the rice in a large bowl of water. Pour off the water, refill and wash again. Repeat a few more times, then drain the rice through a colander. Put into a saucepan with 4 ¼ cups of water. (If you want to follow strict Japanese practice, drain the rice in the colander for 30 minutes and leave the rice to soak in the saucepan for another 30 minutes before cooking.) Bring the rice to the boil with the lid on, then reduce to a simmer and cook until all the water is absorbed. Leave the rice in the saucepan for 15 minutes before tipping into a bowl. Heat the vinegar, salt and sugar until the sugar dissolves and stir this mixture into the rice. Leave to cool to room temperature.

For nigiri, dip your hands in a bowl of water that has a little vinegar in it. Take some rice and mould it into a fat finger. Smear a little wasabi on top of the rice and place a slice of raw fish, prawn or tofu on top of that. For different presentations, wrap the sushi with a strip of nori or top with a diamond of beetroot.

For nori-maki, lay a sheet of nori on a work surface. Wet your hands in the bowl of water and take some rice and spread it over the sheet in a thin layer, leaving about 2 cm (¾ in) free on the sides and 5 cm (2 in) free at the far end. Add any filling you like (for example, spring onion, tuna and beetroot, or any combination your imagination allows) in a horizontal line across the rice. Wet the sides of the nori sheet and roll up. Tuck in the sides and slice the rolls into cross sections.

Wild barramundi in gremolata crumb with lemon and caper mashed potatoes

Potatoes
500 g (1 lb 2 oz) floury potatoes such as Dutch cream,
    Toolangi delight or sebago
½ cup extra-virgin olive oil
½ cup triple cream
1 lemon, zested and juiced
½ cup salted capers, soaked in water for a few minutes
    then rinsed well
salt
cracked white pepper

Barramundi
2 cups Japanese (panko) breadcrumbs
1 cup chopped flat-leaf parsley
1 lemon, zested
3 garlic cloves, finely chopped
4 wild barramundi fillets
1 cup plain (all-purpose) flour
salt and pepper
2 eggs, beaten
extra-virgin olive oil
good mayonnaise (page 191)
lemon wedges

Boil the potatoes whole in salted water until soft. Drain, peel and mash with the olive oil, cream, lemon zest and capers. Stir in the lemon juice and season with salt and pepper. Keep the mash warm.

Combine the breadcrumbs, parsley, lemon zest and garlic in a bowl, mixing well.

Roll the barramundi fillets in flour seasoned with salt and pepper, then dip into the beaten egg. Press into the crumbs, aiming to coat with as many as possible.

Heat some olive oil in a heavy-based frying pan and gently fry the fillets until golden brown on each side.

Come and get it
Spoon the mashed potato onto plates and top with the crumbed barramundi. Serve with mayonnaise and lemon wedges.

The Loss of the Cataraqui

After sailing ships from England rounded the Cape of Good Hope, they pushed deep into the southern latitudes to take advantage of the roaring forties. This was known as the Great Circle Route. The skipper would aim his vessel for the 100-kilometre-wide stretch of water between Cape Otway on mainland Australia and Cape Wickham on King Island, which lies at the western entrance to Bass Strait. Calculating longitude in those days was achieved by chronometer and midday sightings. One clock was set at Greenwich Mean Time; the other was set to local time by sighting the sun at midday. As the earth is twenty-four hours in circumference, the time difference plots one's longitudinal position relative to the prime meridian at Greenwich. A few seconds' error on the clock could put a ship out by miles, which is exactly what happened to Captain Christopher Finlay on 4 August 1845.

It was a filthy night, with howling winds, mountainous black seas and driving rain. Finlay was on the last leg of his journey to the Port of Melbourne, a hundred days into what had been a relatively uneventful voyage. One crewman had gone overboard and was lost at sea. Five babies had been born and six had died. On board were forty crew and 366 assisted emigrants, a large portion being women and children. Finlay had hove to at 7 p.m. the previous evening, to ride out the howling gale, and at 3 a.m. decided to get underway. He had calculated he was some 60 or 70 miles north of King Island, and by maintaining an easterly course he would sight Cape Otway in the morning light. Just ninety minutes later, the *Cataraqui* crashed without warning into a jagged reef 650 feet off the coast of King Island. They were 70 miles south of where Finlay had thought they were.

Water immediately started pouring through the breached hull, and although the ladders had collapsed the crew managed to get more than three hundred terrified emigrants and their children up onto the deck. Many were washed overboard to either drown or be smashed against the rocks by the surf. At around 5 a.m. the ship rolled onto her port side. Attempts to raise her by cutting away the masts were futile, as the hull was full of water. As the sun rose, some two hundred survivors were still desperately clinging to the upturned wreck. The stern of the vessel had washed in, and dead bodies were floating around the ship. With every wave survivors were washed away, relatives parted, children lost. This went on all day long. At around 4 p.m. the ship split in two amidships, and between seventy and a hundred people were taken. An hour later the hull split again, leaving about seventy survivors desperately clinging to the forecastle, the only part of the ship still above water. The remaining crew ran lifelines along the wreck for the survivors to cling to.

Throughout the night, giant waves breached the forecastle and picked off the exhausted survivors piecemeal. At daybreak on 5 August there were but thirty remaining. Early in the morning the last part of the *Cataraqui* broke up completely. Of the 409 people on board, 400 perished. These comprised sixty-two families, thirty-three unmarried women and twenty-two unmarried males. More than half were under twenty-one years of age. Only eight crew and one emigrant—Solomon Brown, a thirty-year-old labourer from Bedfordshire—survived.

Bass Strait 'Constable' David Howie, himself wrecked on King Island, found the castaways the following day, and they set about the grisly task of burying the dead. They buried 342 people in four mass graves, one holding 200. After five weeks, the survivors were picked up by the cutter *Midge* and shipped to Melbourne. To this day the loss of the *Cataraqui* remains Australia's worst civil disaster.

Gefilte fish

Carp—the scourge of Australia's inland waterways—were introduced from Europe; they muddy our waterways and destroy habitat for native species. If you catch one it is illegal to throw it back! We could solve our carp problem if everyone started eating gefilte fish, a classic Jewish recipe. Traditionally, whole fish are cooked, then everything is carefully removed from the skin. The bones are discarded and the flesh is minced and stuffed back in—gefilte means 'stuffed' in Yiddish. Nowadays, the trend is to serve it as patties and broth.

6 kg carp (13 lb), scaled, gutted and filleted to give 3 kg (6 lb 10 oz)
    meat (reserve the heads, skin and bones)
salt
3 onions, chopped
4 medium carrots, peeled
2 tablespoons sugar
4 large eggs
ground black pepper
⅓ cup matzah meal (see Glossary, page 248)
flat-leaf parsley sprigs
fresh horseradish

Place the carp heads, skin and bones in a pot and cover with 3–4 litres (6–8 pints) of water. Add 3 teaspoons of salt. Bring to the boil, skimming the foam from the surface several times. Add one-third of the onions, 3 of the whole carrots and the sugar. Cover with a lid and simmer for 30 minutes – 1 hour.

Mince the fish meat in a food processor and transfer to a bowl. Chop the remaining carrot and add to the processor with the remaining onions. Pulse to a fine mince and add to the fish.

Mix the eggs into the fish mixture one at a time. Gradually add ½ cup of water and season with salt and pepper. Mix in the matzah meal—you should have a light, soft mixture. Shape into oval patties about 7.5 cm (3 in) long.

Strain the stock, reserving the carrots, and return to a simmer. Gently drop the patties into the stock and simmer for 30 minutes, covered with the lid.

Remove the patties with a slotted spoon and arrange on a platter. Slice the carrots and place over the patties. Spoon a little stock on top to moisten the patties and leave to cool. When at room temperature, put in the refrigerator to chill.

Come and get it
Garnish with sprigs of parsley and fine shavings of fresh horseradish. (Or if you can't get fresh, try Newman's in a jar, a South Australian institution!)

Snapper poached in Chinese red stock with stir-fried vegetables

Snapper in stock

200 ml (7 fl oz) mushroom soy sauce

200 ml (7 fl oz) light soy sauce

400 ml (13 fl oz) Chinese rice wine

3 cm (1 in) ginger

3 garlic cloves, smashed

3 dried shiitake mushrooms,
    softened in warm water and
    squeezed dry, stems discarded,
    sliced

100 g (3 ½ oz) yellow rock
    sugar (see Glossary, page 248)

1 cinnamon stick

2 star anise

1 orange, zested

1 litre (2 pints) fish stock (page 2)

snapper fillets (or other firm fish
    such as blue-eye trevalla or
    even tuna)

Vegetables

2 tablespoons peanut oil

1 large shallot, finely chopped

2 garlic cloves, finely chopped

small red chillies to taste, finely
    chopped

1 bunch Chinese broccoli, cut into
    5 cm (2 in) lengths

100 g (3 ½ oz) snow peas

100 g (3 ½ oz) green beans, halved

handful of snow-pea sprouts

handful of bean sprouts

Combine the ingredients for the stock in a large, deep pan except for the fish stock and snapper. Bring to the boil and simmer for 10 minutes, then add the stock, bring back to the boil and simmer for another 5 minutes.

Turn the heat to a gentle simmer and add the snapper. Poach for 4–5 minutes.

While the fish is poaching, stir-fry the vegetables. Heat the peanut oil in a wok and fry the shallot, garlic and chilli until aromatic. Add the Chinese broccoli, snow peas and beans and stir-fry vigorously for 1–2 minutes, until bright green. Add the sprouts and stir-fry for another 10 seconds.

Come and get it

Spoon the vegetables into shallow bowls and top with the fish. Spoon over the poaching liquid.

Blue-eye trevalla with wasabi mashed potatoes and crispy kale

Potatoes
1 head of garlic
1 teaspoon extra-virgin olive oil
1 kg (2 lb 3 oz) floury potatoes such as Dutch cream,
     Toolangi delight or sebago
100 g (3 ½ oz) butter
200 ml (7 fl oz) triple cream
1 cup milk
1 tablespoon wasabi powder
salt

Kale
1 bunch cavolo nero (Tuscan kale), trimmed
⅓ cup extra-virgin olive oil
1 teaspoon flaky salt

Blue-eye trevalla
4 blue-eye trevalla cutlets
plain (all-purpose) flour
salt and pepper
⅓ cup extra-virgin olive oil
1 cup sauvignon blanc
1 lime, juiced
1 tablespoon butter

For the mash, preheat the oven to 180°C (350°F). Brush the garlic with the olive oil and bake for 45 minutes. Slip the cloves out of their skins.

Boil the potatoes whole in salted water until soft. Drain, peel and combine with the garlic, butter and cream. Mash vigorously, slowly adding the milk. Mix the wasabi powder with a little water to form a paste and add to the mash. Season to taste with salt. Keep the mash warm.

Fold the cavolo nero leaves in half vertically like a book and cut out the tough stems. Toss with the olive oil and salt and spread on a baking tray. Roast for 5 minutes, then turn the leaves and roast for a further 5 minutes, or until brown and crisp. Leave to cool.

Roll the cutlets in plain flour seasoned with salt and pepper. Heat the olive oil in a heavy-based frying pan and fry the fillets until golden on each side. Transfer to a non-stick baking tray and keep warm in the oven. Meanwhile, deglaze the frying pan with the wine, lime juice and butter, boiling until reduced by half.

Come and get it
Place a dollop of mash on each plate and top with the fish. Pour over the sauce and garnish with the brittle chips of cavolo nero.

Tempura mulloway with black-bean sauce

Deep-frying was introduced to Japan around 400 years ago by Portuguese and Dutch merchants. The Japanese refined the technique to make light, crisp tempura. In order to get this batter right, you must make it just before frying, and it is essential that you use ice-cold water, which stops the batter becoming sticky. Don't over-mix the batter (a few lumps aren't critical) or over-coat the fish; a light coat is best or it will become oily. The smooth and glossy black-bean sauce contrasts beautifully with the tempura fish.

Sauce
¼ cup peanut oil
5 garlic cloves, crushed
3 cm (1 in) ginger, finely chopped
3 onions, finely chopped
¼ cup fermented black beans, rinsed
½ cup fish or chicken stock
2 tablespoons maltose (see Glossary, page 248)
2 tablespoons tamari soy sauce
2 tablespoons sesame oil
¼ cup kudzu (see Glossary, page 248), dissolved in ½ cup water
2 spring onions (scallions), finely sliced

Tempura mulloway
1 litre (2 pints) peanut oil
1 egg
1 cup ice-cold water
2 tablespoons chilled dry white wine
1 ⅓ cups plain (all-purpose) flour
500 g (1 lb 2 oz) mulloway or other firm white fish, cut into bite-sized chunks
½ teaspoon salt
½ teaspoon ground white pepper

For the sauce, heat the peanut oil in a heavy-based saucepan and fry the garlic, ginger and onion until the onion is starting to soften. Add the black beans and stock and bring to the boil, then stir in the maltose until dissolved. Add the tamari and sesame oil and stir in the kudzu water until thick and glossy. Remove from the heat and stir in the spring onion. Set aside while you prepare the tempura fish.

Heat the oil in a wok to 180°C (350°F). Meanwhile, beat the egg in a bowl until light and fluffy, then gradually add the water and wine. Sift in 1 cup of the flour and quickly whisk to incorporate.

Roll the fish in the remaining flour seasoned with the salt and pepper.

Dip the fish pieces lightly in the batter and shake off any excess. Carefully drop a few pieces at a time into the hot oil and fry until golden brown. Drain on paper towel while you cook the rest.

Come and get it
Reheat the sauce. Place the tempura fish pieces in bowls and spoon dollops of hot sauce on top.

Ian Fairweather

'I've Gone with the Wind'

Beside the clifftop walk near the Northern Territory Museum and Art Gallery in Darwin are a mosaic and plaque commemorating an extraordinary journey undertaken by the well-known artist Ian Fairweather.

Fairweather was born in Scotland in 1891, and educated in London and Switzerland before attending an officer training school in Belfast. He was captured by the Germans soon after the outbreak of World War I and spent the war years as a prisoner of war. On his release, he studied art in Holland, England and Germany before his wanderlust drew him to the Far East. During the 1930s, he moved incessantly across Asia, living in Peking, Tokyo, Formosa, Hong Kong, Jakarta, Brisbane, Cairns, Saigon, Bangkok, Calcutta and Bangalore. He was in India when World War II broke out and, still being on the British Reserve of Officers, entered the army as a captain and served as commandant of a huge camp near Bangalore that housed Italian prisoners of war. He was discharged from the army in 1943 and returned to Australia, where he faded into obscurity, and perhaps would have remained there had it not been for an extraordinary escapade which brought him the attention of the international media.

In 1952, Fairweather had drifted to Darwin. He was sixty-one years old. At first he lived in an abandoned railway truck, then in the hull of a derelict patrol vessel lying on the beach. He began constructing a raft using the belly tanks of three aircraft and a deck of driftwood, and, on 29 April, with 4 gallons of water and a meagre supply of food, he put to sea. Some 30 miles offshore he was hailed by a pearling lugger that offered to tow him back to Darwin. He declined. Instead, he said, 'I'm going to Timor. Is this the right road?' The captain of the lugger was astonished. On his return to Darwin he alerted the authorities, as Timor was 500 miles away! A search by planes and ships failed to locate the raft, and Fairweather was given up as lost at sea.

Sixteen days later, having survived storms and the attentions of schools of man-eating sharks, badly burnt from the incessant tropical sun and dehydrated, Fairweather went ashore at West Timor, and was subsequently arrested by Indonesian authorities. Later he said:

> I made the trip because I wanted to get to Portuguese Timor, as the next best thing to Bali where I'd done the best painting in my life, in the months I was there after coming out of China twenty years or so before. Unfortunately, my raft went ashore in Indonesian Timor, and the Indonesians were being very aggressive and nationalistic just then. They took me to Bali, but I was a white man and they had to make a propaganda show of me. They didn't knock me about, but it was all rather ghastly.

Released after three months, he was deported to Singapore, and thence to England. He tried to sell a manuscript and drawings of his journey, but the deal fell through. Later he sent them to a literary agent in Paris, who returned the manuscript but not the drawings. He took a job labouring, digging ditches in a Devonshire bog, eventually scraping together enough money for a passage back to Australia. During the journey he hurled his manuscript overboard, later stating, 'It was a rotten book anyway. I only mourned the drawings. One of them was not too bad'.

Fairweather finally settled on Bribie Island, where he constructed some thatched huts to live in and continue his painting. His works now hang in all the state galleries in Australia, as well as the Tate and Leicester galleries in London and the Ulster Museum in Belfast.

Fish and chips

When I was a child, the Friday night dinner ritual was performed at a concrete table on the local foreshore. Beneath the banksias and shiny leaf, on a carpet of couch grass, our fish and chips would come wrapped in newspaper, usually the Melbourne *Herald*, a broadsheet in those days. My sister and I would each have a crunchy piece of battered flake and we'd share the chips between us. We'd eat the crunchy ones along with all the 'scratchings, scrobblings and gribblings' (colourful British terminology for the crunchy scraps of batter that would fall into the hot fat). We'd toss the soggy chips to the raucous flock of seagulls that always appeared out of nowhere.

Mum and Dad would chow down on a bright-red boiled lobster, cracking the legs to extract the sweet white meat and dipping it into a jar of mayonnaise. In those days, lobsters were cheap and also came wrapped in newspaper. Sometimes we kids would get treated to a lobster leg, although we did prefer our chips. There was something slimy about the lobster—it didn't have the right mouth-feel for a six year old.

Sometimes we'd be rugged up against a bone-chilling south-westerly that whipped the bay's water into white horses; other times the evening would be balmy and still, and after dinner we'd run out to the edge of the sandbanks, stomachs full, mouths oily, not a care in the world.

At some indeterminate point, things changed. Fish and chips no longer tasted so good. Beef dripping and lard were replaced by commercial vegetable oil, which was much better for you but simply didn't have the same flavour. Fish and chip shops stopped making their own chips, instead ordering them in, pre-fried and frozen. Even the fish was no longer fresh or freshly battered, but frozen and mushy, and if the proprietor manning the fryer removed the fish too soon, it had a disgusting uncooked inner layer of commercial batter with an indescribable flavour; it certainly didn't relate to anything edible. To add insult to injury, the whole catastrophe is nowadays blanketed in a dusting of 'chicken salt': an evil blend of salt, artificial flavours and flavour enhancers that leave your taste buds shrivelled and your mouth dehydrated.

The good news is that you can enjoy delicious fish and chips at home so long as a few simple rules are adhered to. Your oil must be fresh and top quality: Chinese pure peanut oil is as good as any. It must be heated to the correct temperature of 180–190°C (350–375°F). You must heat sufficient quantities of oil in a large enough pot so that it doesn't overflow or drop in temperature when you put the fish in it. Your batter must be left long enough to start fermenting, and must be kept chilled. Your potatoes must be fresh, firm and a floury variety: I like russet Burbank and Toolangi delight. After being sliced, they must be soaked in salted water to remove their starch, then patted dry. They must be cooked twice, and be well drained. Adhere to these rules and you will be in fish-and-chip heaven!

While the method itself should be followed carefully, there is room for interpretation in the ingredients. For instance, I prefer my fish in bite-sized pieces rather than whole fillets. You can even wrap the fish in Japanese nori if you like, and as well as potato chips, there are plenty of other vegetables that can be fried and even battered if you wish; just make sure you slice root vegetables thinly enough. And if you have any leftover cooked rice in the refrigerator, you can make rice balls: roll the rice into balls with finely chopped onion and a little ginger, then coat in sesame seeds and fry. As for condiments and sides, there is vinegar of course, or I like to mix 1 cup of shredded daikon with 2 finely chopped pickled Japanese umeboshi plums, which cuts the oil just like vinegar.

Fish and chips (continued)

1 ½ cups plain (all-purpose) flour, plus extra for coating the fish
½ cup cornflour (cornstarch)
1 teaspoon bicarbonate of soda
salt
1 cup cold Coopers ale
1 cup cold soda water
sesame seeds (optional)
floury potatoes such as russet Burbank or Toolangi delight
fish fillets cut into bite-sized pieces
soy sauce
fish sauce
3 litres (6 pints) peanut oil (I use the Lion and Globe brand from China)
flaky salt to serve

Sift the flours into a bowl and add the bicarbonate of soda and 1 teaspoon of salt. Stir well. Slowly whisk in the ale and soda water to form a thin batter. Cover with a damp tea towel and refrigerate for at least 1 hour. The batter may need to be thinned further, as it tends to thicken a little when left to stand; if so, thin with more ale. Add a good handful of sesame seeds if desired.

Cut the potatoes into chips (I leave the skin on) and soak in salted cold water for 30 minutes to remove the starch, changing the water a couple of times. Drain and pat dry with a tea towel.

Meanwhile, marinate the fish pieces in a little soy and fish sauce for about 30 minutes. (Or you can use any manner of marinades—various sauces, lime or lemon juice.)

Heat the oil in a large pot fitted with a deep-frying basket to 190°C (375°F). Place the chips in the basket and gently immerse into the oil, being careful that the oil doesn't overflow. The chips should bubble vigorously and the delightful aroma of roasting peanuts should fill the room. Cook until just coloured and remove from the oil. Allow to drain and cool slightly.

Meanwhile, roll the fish in plain flour then dip into the batter and place in the hot oil. Cook until golden. As you're cooking the fish, remember to constantly scoop out the scraps of batter (the scratchings, scrobblings and gribblings) to keep the oil clean. Drain the fish on paper towel.

Immerse the chips in the oil again and cook until they turn a delicious golden brown and are crunchy at the edges. Remove from the oil, drain well and toss in flaky salt.

Come and get it
I like to serve my fish and chips in a traditional basket.

Keeping your oil
If you don't burn your oil and you keep it well strained, it will keep for a month or so in a sealed bottle. A Japanese umeboshi plum will help preserve it.

Flathead tortellini with fragrant green sauce

If you have a day to spend in the kitchen before your guests arrive for dinner, then this is an exquisite starter; trouble is, it's a hard act to follow!

Filling

500 g (1 lb 2 oz) boneless flathead
    fillets
2 tablespoons fish sauce
2 tablespoons peanut oil
2 cm (¾ in) ginger, finely chopped
3 garlic cloves, finely chopped
3 spring onions (scallions), finely
    sliced
1 tablespoon Chinese rice wine
1 tablespoon light soy sauce or
    shoyu
1 lime, zested
1 teaspoon salt

Sauce

2 small green chillies
⅓ cup chopped coriander (cilantro)
⅓ cup chopped basil
⅓ cup chopped Vietnamese mint
3 spring onions (scallions), green
    tops only, chopped
2 tablespoons peanut oil
1 teaspoon sesame oil
2 garlic cloves, chopped
2 cm (¾ in) ginger, chopped
1 tablespoon Chinese brown bean
    paste (see Glossary, page 248)
1 tablespoon sugar
1 tablespoon Chinese rice wine
½ cup fish stock (page 2)
1 tablespoon oyster sauce
100 g (3 ½ oz) butter, cubed

Dough

2 cups plain (all-purpose) flour
2 extra-large eggs
1 ½ tablespoons extra-virgin olive oil
salt
coriander (cilantro) leaves

Mince the flathead. Combine in a bowl with the fish sauce.

Heat the peanut oil in a frying pan and fry the ginger and garlic until fragrant. Add the spring onions, fry, then add the flathead and stir-fry gently until cooked through. Add the rice wine, soy sauce, lime zest and salt and remove from the heat. Cool.

For the sauce, combine the chillies, coriander, basil, Vietnamese mint and spring onions in a food processor and blend to a paste.

In a wok, heat the oils and fry the garlic, ginger and bean paste until fragrant. Add the sugar, rice wine and herb paste and simmer for a couple of minutes. Strain through a fine sieve, extracting as much of the juice as possible. Return to the wok, add the fish stock and oyster sauce, and reduce by a third. Set aside.

For the dough, mound the flour on a work surface and make a well in the middle. Crack the eggs into the well and add the oil and a pinch of salt. Using a fork, mix the eggs and oil together, gradually incorporating the flour. Keep incorporating the flour with your hands until you have a smooth dough. Set aside to rest.

Cut the dough in half and roll one piece through a pasta machine at its widest setting. Keep rolling through until the second-finest setting is reached and you have a long, thin pasta sheet. Place on a lightly floured surface and roll out the other piece of dough. Place coriander leaves on the bottom halves of the pasta sheets and fold the top halves over. Run the sheets through the pasta machine on its finest setting.

Place level teaspoons of the flathead mixture in rows along the length of one pasta sheet, 5 cm (2 in) apart. Lay the second sheet over the top and with the tips of your fingers, press around the edges and down the centre of the sheet. Cut into rectangles with a pastry cutter or a sharp knife. Press around the rectangles to ensure a good seal.

Bring 3 litres (6 pints) of water to a rolling boil and add 2 tablespoons of salt. Meanwhile, gently warm some serving plates. Cook the tortellini for 30 seconds – 2 minutes. Remove with a slotted spoon and put 3–4 on each plate.

While the pasta is cooking, return the sauce to a rapid boil and quickly whisk in the butter.

Come and get it
Spoon the sauce over the tortellini and garnish with extra coriander.

SHELLS

Green-lipped mussels with balsamic vinegar

New Zealand green-lipped mussels have very tender meat and a sweet flavour. A balsamic-vinegar reduction combines superbly to create an easy and memorable dish.

½ cup balsamic vinegar
2 kg (4 lb 6 oz) green-lipped mussels, cleaned and
    de-bearded
3 spring onions (scallions), finely sliced

Put the balsamic vinegar in a saucepan and boil until reduced by half. Leave to cool.

Place the mussels in a single layer in a large bamboo steamer and place over a wok of boiling water. Steam for 5–8 minutes, until the shells open. (Rather than automatically discarding any that don't, I prise the closed ones open and carefully inspect them; you often find a perfectly healthy mussel inside.)

Come and get it
Sprinkle the reduced balsamic vinegar over the mussels and garnish with the spring onion. As simple as that!

Oysters

George Vancouver was one of the early European fans of Australian oysters. He happened upon them in Albany in 1791 and wrote:

> Found a passage, narrow and shoal for some distance, into the north-eastern harbour; where a bar was found to extend across its entrance, on which there was only 3 fathoms of water … In our way out of this harbour, the boats grounded on a bank we had not before perceived; this was covered with oysters of a most delicious flavour, on which we sumptuously regaled; and, loading in about half an hour, the boats for our friends on board, we commemorated the discovery by calling it Oyster Harbour.

Of course, Aboriginal Australians had been eating oysters for thousands of years, as evidenced by the numerous shell middens scattered around the coast.

The oyster's aphrodisiac powers are legendary. Giacomo Casanova, legendary lover of women, wrote: 'I placed the shell on the edge of her lips and after a good deal of laughing, she sucked in the oyster, which she held between her lips. I instantly recovered it by placing my lips on hers'.

Roman emperors paid for oysters with their weight in gold. Jonathan Swift (1667–1745) was less enamoured and wrote: 'He was a bold man that first ate an oyster'. The texture can certainly be challenging to the initiate. I was introduced to oysters as a child; I love them, they taste like the sea. I eat them freshly shucked with little, if any, enhancement, but here are a few serving ideas:

- A squeeze of lemon juice and some crusty bread.
- A few drops of balsamic vinegar that has been reduced by half.
- A little finely chopped red onion and a splash of good balsamic vinegar.
- A salsa of capsicum (bell pepper), coriander (cilantro) and shallots in a dressing of extra-virgin olive oil, red-wine vinegar and lime juice.
- A spoonful of arame salad (page 194).
- A few gratings of fresh horseradish.
- A vinaigrette of rice vinegar, soy sauce, sugar, grated ginger, lemon juice and light-flavoured oil.
- In a shot glass with vodka, tomato juice, lemon, Tabasco sauce and cracked pepper (a bloody Mary).
- A dressing of fish sauce, lime juice, chilli, very finely sliced lemongrass and a little sugar and fresh coriander (cilantro), topped with fried shallots.
- A small dollop of organic triple cream and half a teaspoon of salmon roe.
- A drizzle of Japanese ponzu sauce, garnished with a thatch of deep-fried leek strands.
- A classic mignonette: ⅔ cup of red-wine vinegar, 3 minced shallots, ½ teaspoon of cracked pepper and a pinch of salt, chilled.

Pipis with basil and Thai chilli paste

This is my brother-in-law Cha's signature dish—well, almost everything he cooks is a signature dish! For Thai men, as for Italian men, cooking is cultural; something you just do. This dish is very quick to prepare and delicious to eat. The important thing is to keep the pipis moist with the stock or water while they're cooking.

1 kg (2 lb 3 oz) pipis in their shells (or you can use cockles or mussels)
2 tablespoons peanut oil
4–5 garlic cloves, smashed with the skin on
2 shallots, smashed with the skin on
1 cup chicken stock or water
1 heaped tablespoon Thai chilli paste (see Glossary, page 248)
2 teaspoons grated palm sugar
small red chillies to taste (the dish is supposed to be quite hot), sliced
2 tablespoons fish sauce
small handful of Thai basil leaves

Soak the pipis in a container filled with sea water, or water with sea salt added at 35 g (1 ¼ oz) per litre (2 pints), for 1 hour. Vigorously knock the container every so often—this causes the pipis to release any sand or grit.

Heat the oil in a wok and stir-fry the garlic and shallots until fragrant. Turn up the heat and add the pipis. Stir briefly, then cover with a lid, lifting it every 10 seconds or so to give the pipis another stir. Gradually add the stock or water as the wok dries out. When the pipis have opened, remove the lid and stir in the chilli paste, palm sugar, chillies and fish sauce.

Come and get it

Transfer to a serving bowl and scatter with the basil.

Rather than automatically discarding any pipis that didn't open, I prise the closed ones open and carefully inspect them; you often find a perfectly healthy pipi inside.

The Loch Ard

'Midst darkness, dashing through the spray
The vessel cuts her headlong way
Ill fated ship 'Loch Ard.'
She spreads her canvass to the wind,
All hope her haven so to find—
'Alas! How hope is marred'.
Black Boreas bade the tempest rise,
And onward through the foam she flies,
Till lost to all command.

Thos Shepherd, *Geelong Times*

On a calm day, Victoria's Shipwreck Coast is a wild, rugged place; however, when the sea is running, it is both beautiful and terrifying, as you brace against the bone-chilling winds blowing up from the Southern Ocean. The sea boils and foams in a white maelstrom beneath cliffs that look as though they have been carved in anger by the chisel of some giant mason. On the far tip of Muttonbird Island is the place where, on a dark winter's night in 1878, a scene of gothic horror was played out as the *Loch Ard*, in the final hours of her ninety-day journey from England, smashed into the cliffs and sank beneath the waves, taking fifty-two souls with her to the bottom. Only two people survived: the ship's apprentice Tom Pierce, and eighteen-year-old Eva Carmichael. Eva's father, suffering from tuberculosis, had decided to immigrate to Queensland with his wife and six of their seven children.

Loch Line ships were among the first to use steel instead of wood in the construction of their hulls and lower masts, and they quickly earnt a reputation for stability and comfort. But sixteen of their twenty-three vessels met with disaster at sea. The *Loch Ard* was built in Glasgow in 1873 and during her short career survived a number of near misses. She once arrived in Melbourne after sailing for forty-six days under a jury rig, her masts having collapsed during a fierce storm in the middle of the Indian Ocean.

The *Loch Ard* sailed for Melbourne from Gravesend on 1 March 1878. The ship's master was George Gibb, who had been recently married and was just twenty-nine years old. At noon on 31 May, at the westerly entrance to Bass Strait, the officers on the poop took their final sightings to determine longitude, but the sky was hazy and the fix poor. The ship's chronometers were suspect. Gibb was therefore preparing to thread the needle not entirely sure of his ship's position. His unease was obvious that evening, as he elected to remain with his officers of the watch rather than attend the end-of-voyage party below decks. There were stars above and to the south, but a heavy fog obscured the north. At midnight a lead was cast and 63 fathoms recorded. Gibb ordered the sail to be taken in to slow the ship, and every fifteen minutes sent a man aloft to search for the Cape Otway light.

At 4 a.m. the haze suddenly lifted, and dead ahead in the darkness loomed high, rugged limestone cliffs. From the mast came the cry all sailors dread: 'Breakers ahead!' Gibb swung into action. With a cool head he called for more sail and brought the ship round to starboard. He couldn't gain enough speed and she swung back to port. To try and prevent the ship from drifting into the rocks, Gibb ordered both anchors be let go with fifty fathoms of chain. Alas, they dragged along the bottom, but at least they brought her head back to the wind. In a textbook manoeuvre, Gibb ordered the yardarms braced to a port tack and the anchors slipped. Just when it seemed she was gaining headway, there was a 'fearful shuddering crash' as the great ship struck a ledge on her starboard quarter. The collision was of such intensity that the top deck was rent from the hull. At that same moment, the topmast collapsed onto the deck, 'striking in its passage two seamen and carrying them overboard, one appearing to be struck dead on the spot'.

On deck a wild, confused scene ensued. With each roll of the waves the ship's yardarms crashed into the unstable limestone cliffs above, sending boulders careening down onto the deck. The apprentice Tom Pierce struggled to launch a lifeboat, but it capsized with Tom underneath, and he was dragged out to sea. Meanwhile, Eva Carmichael had reached the poop deck. Gibb put his arms around her and calmly said, 'If you are saved, Eva, let my dear wife know that I died like a sailor'. Within moments a breaker crashed over the deck and Eva was swept into the icy black sea.

Tom Pierce floated away beneath the upturned lifeboat, eventually through the narrow entrance to what is now known as Loch Ard Gorge, and some hours later hauled himself wet and cold onto the beach. Eva had grabbed on to a chicken coop that was floating amid the flotsam and jetsam. She later said, 'God taught me to swim in my distressed plight for I had never swum before'. She also eventually drifted into the gorge.

Tom was sifting through the wreckage that had come ashore looking for something to eat when he heard a woman's scream. Thinking it was coming from above he looked up, but he soon realised it was from the sea. Although exhausted, he swam out and brought the barely conscious girl to shore. In all probability she had been in the water for more than five hours. He took her to a cave by the beach and, finding a case of brandy, opened a bottle. She drank some; he rubbed some on her body and then drank the rest himself. Exhausted, Eva fell into a stupor; Tom left her and went to scale the gorge to raise help.

He staggered westward towards Warrnambool and was eventually spotted, wet, bruised and dazed, by a stockman from nearby Glenample Station. As word filtered through to Melbourne, crowds of sightseers began arriving to gaze down from the cliffs at the bodies and debris that were washing up on the beaches. The police attempted to control those with more sinister intentions: wreckers and thieves who abseiled down the cliffs, often under the cover of darkness, to plunder and loot the bounty below. Protected from the media scrum and the public eye, Eva remained at Gelnample, recuperating. Tom was awarded a gold watch, and returned to sea a celebrated hero. He went on to survive further shipwrecks, and although they corresponded once or twice, he and Eva never met again.

When Eva had recovered sufficiently to return to Europe, she did so by steam, the ticket paid for by a Melbourne benefit. The tragic loss of the *Loch Ard* signalled the end of passenger-carrying sailing ships on the Australian run. It was the final nail in the coffin for clipper ships: economic prudence and the public desire for safer travel on the seas heralded in the era of the steamship.

There is a lonely little cemetery beside Loch Ard Gorge where Eva Carmichael's family is buried, along with those crew and passengers whose bodies eventually washed up on shore. It is a strangely peaceful place, tucked in the coastal heath and grassland, not far from the roar of the sea, a sanctuary amid so much violence.

Moules à la marinière

This is a timeless and classic French way to cook mussels, and also very simple. It is excellent with New Zealand green-lipped, but also I love it with the Australian blue mussel. If you like, you can take an extra step after the mussels have been cooked and dip them in batter and deep-fry them.

2 kg (4 lb 6 oz) mussels, cleaned and de-bearded
1 onion, finely chopped
1 shallot, finely chopped
1 garlic clove, finely chopped
2 thyme sprigs
2 flat-leaf parsley sprigs, plus extra chopped parsley to garnish
50 g (2 oz) butter
1 cup dry riesling
crusty bread

Combine all the ingredients except the bread in a large saucepan and cook over fairly high heat for around 5 minutes, until the mussels have opened. (Rather than automatically discarding any that don't, I prise the closed ones open and carefully inspect them; you often find a perfectly healthy mussel inside.)

Come and get it
Transfer the mussels to serving bowls. Strain the cooking liquid over the top and sprinkle with chopped parsley. Serve with crusty bread.

Cockles in the sand

Make this when you are in a place where you can collect cockles from the beach. Once you have collected them, put them in a bucket of sea water, and every so often give the bucket a kick. This will make the cockles spit out any grit they may have in them; they will be ready to cook after an hour or so.

This method of cooking cockles in the sand is a traditional Aboriginal way and works well with any bi-valve mollusc (mussels, scallops and the like). Burying the shells in wet sand prevents them from opening when cooking, retaining their flavour and preventing sand and grit getting in. Always be careful as hot and cold sand are the same colour so you can easily get a nasty burn. When you have finished cooking, bury the hot sand to clean up the site and prevent anyone with bare feet from burning themselves.

The recipe includes two Asian sauces, but you might prefer to choose just one and increase the quantity.

Lime sauce
2 limes, juiced
1 tablespoon fish sauce
1 teaspoon palm sugar
10 coriander (cilantro) leaves
finely chopped red chilli to taste

Sweet soy sauce
¼ cup kecap manis (sweet soy sauce)
1 tablespoon soy sauce
6 drops of sesame oil
finely chopped red chilli to taste

2 kg (4 lb 6 oz) cockles

Combine the sauce ingredients in bowls and set aside.

Bury the cockles halfway in moist sand near the water's edge, with their hinges facing up. Light a small twig fire over the top of them. They should take 5–10 minutes to cook and open.

Come and get it
When the cockles are done, brush the ash and sand from them. Dip the meat into the sauce and enjoy.

Marinated oyster and smoked salmon salad over bitter greens

The flavour of the oysters and smoked salmon infuses with the olive oil to create striking balance and complexity. The refreshing salad is perfect to serve outdoors on a sunny day.

meat from 24 freshly shucked oysters
500 g (1 lb 2 oz) smoked salmon, sliced into strips
¾ cup extra-virgin olive oil
1 lemon, juiced
1 fennel bulb, finely sliced
250 g (9 oz) snow peas
4 large ripe tomatoes, chopped
2 avocados, finely sliced
leaves of flavoursome greens such as endive, rocket (arugula)
    or watercress
flaky salt and cracked pepper
some finely sliced red onion
handful of flat-leaf parsley leaves

Combine the oysters, salmon, olive oil and lemon juice in a bowl and allow the flavours to infuse for a few minutes.

Add the fennel, snow peas, tomato, avocado and bitter greens. Toss together and season to taste.

Come and get it
Spoon the salad onto plates, ensuring there are oysters and salmon on top. Garnish with red onion, parsley and cracked pepper.

Mussels with tomato, preserved lemon and saffron

Success with this colourful dish will rely on your choice of ingredients—the freshest mussels, the best tomatoes (preferably straight from your summer garden) and good-quality dry white wine such as a crisp riesling from the Clare Valley.

200 ml (7 fl oz) extra-virgin olive oil
2 onions, finely chopped
6 garlic cloves, finely chopped
small red chillies to taste, finely chopped
1 kg (2 lb 3 oz) tomatoes (ox heart are good), peeled,
    seeded and roughly chopped
1 preserved lemon, skin only, rinsed and finely sliced
pinch of saffron threads
2 kg (4 lb 6 oz) mussels, cleaned and de-bearded
200 ml (7 fl oz) dry white wine at room temperature
chopped flat-leaf parsley
crusty bread

Heat half of the olive oil in a frying pan and fry the onion, garlic and chilli until the onion is starting to soften. Add the tomatoes, preserved lemon and saffron and gently simmer for 5 minutes until the tomatoes are soft.

Meanwhile, heat the remaining olive oil in a large saucepan until very hot. Add the mussels and wine. Put a lid on, turn the heat down to a fast simmer and cook for 5 minutes, occasionally giving the pan a shake.

Pour the tomato sauce over the mussels and simmer for a further 5 minutes.

Come and get it
Spoon the mussels and sauce into bowls. Garnish with parsley and serve with crusty bread.

Rather than automatically discarding any mussels that didn't open, I prise the closed ones open and carefully inspect them; you often find a perfectly healthy mussel inside.

The Girl from Botany Bay

It's a very desparate attempt to go in an open Boat for a run of about 16 or 17 hundred Leags and in pertacalar for a woman and two small children.

Private John Easty, First Fleet marine

Mary Bryant's epic escape from Botany Bay would have to be one of the great escape stories of all time. The daughter of a Cornish mariner, she was twenty-one years old when she was sentenced to death at the Exeter Assizes for stealing 'a bonnet and other goods' from one Agnes Lakeman in Plymouth. This was commuted to seven years' transportation, and, after a stint on the hulk *Dunkirk* off Plymouth, Mary found herself on the First Fleet, sailing to Australia aboard the *Charlotte*. Before reaching Cape Town she delivered a baby girl, who was baptised Charlotte Spence, and four days after arriving in Port Jackson she married William Bryant, a Cornish fisherman-cum-smuggler who had been transported for resisting arrest at the hands of excise officers. They were one of the first couples to receive a European-style wedding in Australia.

The starving colony needed a fisherman, so Bryant was put in charge of the dinghies that daily cast nets in the harbour. Bryant's position gave him privilege—a hut and a vegetable garden tended by convicts—but it appears the idea of selling fish on the black market instead of handing it all in to the government stores was too tempting for the Cornish smuggler. He was caught and given 100 lashes. Afterwards, while no longer in control of fishing, his skills ensured that he stayed on the boats. In April 1790, Mary gave birth to a boy, Emanuel.

It appears that after his flogging Bryant started planning his escape. News would have reached Port Jackson about William Bligh's extraordinary journey across the Pacific in the *Bounty*'s launch. In 1791, Watkin Tench wrote, 'After the escape of Captain Bligh, no length of passage, or hazard of navigation seemed above human accomplishment'. Bryant could steal a boat, but he had no navigational equipment or weapons. As luck would have it, a Dutch trader, the *Waaksamheyd*, arrived with stores from Batavia. The captain, Detmer Smit, may not have had much respect for the British penal code, for he gave Bryant a compass, a quadrant, a chart of the coast from Port Jackson to Timor, food and muskets. Bryant hid his contraband in rolls of bark beneath the floorboards of his hut and set about forming a plan. The authorities suspected that he was planning an escape and watched him very closely; however, when a squall in February 1791 almost wrecked the governor's six-oar cutter, it gave Bryant the opportunity to refit it with a new mast and prepare it for an ocean voyage.

In March, HMS *Supply* was dispatched to Norfolk Island, and the *Waaksamheyd* sailed for Europe; there was not a ship in Port Jackson capable of giving chase. It was now or never. On a dark, moonless night, Bryant, Mary, their infant children and seven crewmen slipped the boat into the water at Bennelong and then out into the inky blackness. The lookout at South Head missed them, and the tiny boat entered the Pacific Ocean and steered a course northward, up the coast.

At first the seas were kind and they caught plenty of fish, but once north of Port Macquarie they were blown out to sea; 'making no harbour or Creek for nere three weeks we were much distress'd for water and food'. They faced mountainous waves and driving rain. At one point they managed to go ashore at what may have been Moreton Bay, but were soon blown back out to sea. For several more days they battled against the elements,

> thinking every moment to be the last, the sea Coming in so heavy upon us every now and then that two Hands was obliged to keep Bailing out ... I will leave you to Consider what distress we must be in, the Woman and the two little Babies was in a bad condition, everything being so wet.

But the weather eventually abated, and they rounded Cape York. Although entirely coincidental, Bryant's timing could not have been better. He was in the Arafura Sea at the time of year when a stiff south-east trade wind blows, and this drove them under sail all the way to Timor. They avoided being eaten by natives whom, they correctly assumed were cannibals, and against all probability sailed into Coupang on 5 June 1791, passing themselves off to the Dutch governor as survivors of a shipwreck on the Australian coast. It had taken them sixty-nine days to sail 3500 miles.

The governor showed them great hospitality, clothing and housing them, and filling their bellies, but after a couple of months, perhaps due to drunkenness, Bryant confessed the truth, and they were all incarcerated in the fort.

In mid September another group of shipwrecked English sailors under the command of the infamous Captain Edward Edwards rowed into Coupang. The Dutch must have thought that the British had a penchant for extraordinary ocean voyages in small open boats.

In that pestilential city, William Bryant and little Emanuel died of fever. Three of Bryant's crew members died at sea on the journey to Cape Town, where the remaining four, along with Mary and Charlotte, were taken aboard the *Gorgon*, a man-of-war that was returning to England from Australia. On 5 May 1792, little Charlotte died and was buried at sea.

On arrival back in England, Mary was committed to Newgate, in all likelihood to be transported back to Australia. Mary's story found its way into the press, where she was affectionately dubbed 'the girl from Botany Bay'. Her story reached James Boswell, Dr Samuel Johnson's biographer, who pleaded her case to Home Secretary Dundas and Under Secretary of State Evan Nepean. In May 1793 she received an unconditional pardon. Her original seven-year sentence had expired just six weeks earlier. Mary returned to Cornwall and faded into obscurity. Interestingly, the memorandum of the boat journey, written by the navigator James Martin, was given to Jeremy Bentham, the English social reformer and author of *Panopticon versus New South Wales* (1812). The memorandum was lost until it turned up in Bentham's papers in the 1930s.

Razorfish and warrigal greens

Razorfish are shellfish that grow in the mangrove tidal flats of Spencer Gulf and Gulf St Vincent in South Australia, but you can substitute scallops, as pictured here. Warrigal greens are better known as New Zealand spinach, and were named by Captain Cook who first discovered it on the shores of New Zealand. Despite its name, the plant is understood to have originated in Australia and later spread to New Zealand. It occurs all over Australia, both on the coast and in the outback. Joseph Banks took it back to England where it was known as Botany Bay greens and became very popular. It appeared in European and American seed catalogues in the 1820s and is still grown in market gardens outside Paris.

Lime and verjuice sauce
250 g (9 oz) butter
6 shallots, finely chopped
300 ml (10 fl oz) verjuice or chardonnay
2 limes, zested and juiced
salt and pepper

Warrigal greens
50 g (2 oz) unsalted butter
300 g (10 ½ oz) warrigal greens (or use regular spinach)
freshly grated nutmeg
salt and pepper

Razorfish
18 razorfish
2 limes, zested and juiced
salt
1 tablespoon extra-virgin olive oil

For the sauce, heat a small amount of the butter in a saucepan and fry the shallots until starting to soften. Add the verjuice or chardonnay and boil until reduced by a third. Whisk in the remaining butter and add the lime zest and juice and salt and pepper. Keep warm.

For the warrigal greens, heat the butter in a wok until lightly browned, then add the greens, nutmeg and salt and pepper. Cook until the greens have wilted, then tip into a bowl.

Toss the razorfish with the lime zest and juice in a bowl. Season with salt. Heat the oil in the wok and quickly sear the razorfish.

Come and get it
Spoon the greens onto plates and top with the razorfish and sauce.

Seared scallops, silken tofu and Chinese broccoli

3 cups peanut oil
500 g (1 lb 2 oz) silken tofu
½ cup cornflour (cornstarch), plus
    1 tablespoon extra
½ teaspoon salt
1 tablespoon sesame oil
12 scallops with roe
4 garlic cloves, finely chopped
5 cm (2 in) ginger, finely chopped
2 spring onions (scallions), finely chopped
2 bunches Chinese broccoli, bases trimmed, cut in thirds
¼ cup chicken stock
2 tablespoons light soy sauce
2 tablespoons oyster sauce
steamed rice

Heat the oil in a wok to 190°C (375°F). Meanwhile, carefully cut the tofu into bite-sized cubes and gently roll in ½ cup of cornflour seasoned with salt. Deep-fry until golden brown and drain on paper towel.

Mix the extra cornflour and sesame oil with ¼ cup of water.

Strain the deep-frying oil into a heatproof bowl or saucepan and return ¼ cup to the wok. Heat the oil then add the scallops and stir-fry for 30 seconds. Remove and drain on paper towel.

Add another ¼ cup of the oil to the wok and stir-fry the garlic, ginger and spring onions until fragrant. Add the Chinese broccoli and stir-fry until the stems start softening, then add the chicken stock, soy and oyster sauce and stir-fry for another 30 seconds.

Add the cornflour mixture and stir quickly until glossy. Turn the heat down to low and add the scallops and tofu and gently incorporate.

Come and get it
Serve on steamed rice.

Turkish stuffed mussels (*Midye dolması*)

If you are lucky, you can still find mussels growing wild around the Australian coastline. I remember picking them off jetty pylons in Port Phillip as a child—those days are long gone, and the mussels that do grow there now are not safe to eat. (Perhaps they weren't back then either, but I'm still alive!) This dish is served on the streets of Istanbul, particularly on the banks of the Bosphorus River. The flavour of the rice in the shell of the mussel with all its juices is sublime.

½ cup extra-virgin olive oil
3 onions, finely chopped
1 cup rice
⅓ cup pine nuts
⅓ cup currants
½ cup chopped flat-leaf parsley
salt and pepper
36 large mussels, cleaned and de-bearded
3 lemons, juiced
extra lemon wedges

Heat the oil in a saucepan and fry the onions until translucent. Add the rice and fry gently for 20 minutes.

Add 2 cups of boiling water and the pine nuts and currants and cook, covered, until the liquid is absorbed. Stir in the parsley and remove from the heat. Season to taste and leave to cool.

Meanwhile, carefully prise the mussel shells open, keeping the hinges intact. Soak in a bowl of salted water while the rice cools.

Stuff the mussels with the rice mixture and tie them shut with string. Place them in a saucepan and cover with boiling water. Cook gently for half an hour, then drain off the liquid, leaving the mussels to cool to room temperature.

Come and get it
Arrange the mussels on a platter. Squeeze over the lemon juice and serve with extra lemon wedges.

Cantonese braised greenlip abalone and black moss

The southern coast of Australia produces the most wonderful greenlip abalone. On remote beaches in South Australia and Tasmania, incredibly, you can still obtain the prized shellfish with just a snorkel and a knife, metres from the shore.

People often tell me that eating abalone is like chewing on a car tyre: rubbery and flavourless. Nothing could be further from the truth, but the secret is in the cooking. Like game, it should be cooked either fast and furious or slow and gentle. If you get it wrong it is unforgiving, but get it right and the result is sublime. Dried abalone is highly regarded by the Chinese, who believe eating it delays senility and increases fertility. Fresh abalone is a symbol of wealth and is served on very special occasions. The fine strands of black moss represent the fur of pandas or the feathers of the phoenix. This dish is usually served to celebrate Chinese New Year.

1 cup peanut oil
400 g (14 oz) fresh greenlip abalone meat
750 ml (7 fl oz) chicken stock
2 slices of ginger
4 spring onions (scallions), roughly chopped
30 g (1 oz) dried black moss (see Glossary, page 248)
⅓ teaspoon sugar
2 teaspoons cornflour (cornstarch)
1 cup water
leaves of 1 celtuce (Chinese lettuce—wo sun) or cos (romaine) lettuce
2 ½ tablespoons oyster sauce
1 teaspoon light soy sauce
1 teaspoon dark soy sauce

Heat the oil in a wok until hot, then drop in the abalone and very briefly seal on both sides. Remove from the oil and rinse in warm water. Tip out all but ¼ cup of the oil from the wok and set aside.

Heat the chicken stock with the ginger and half of the spring onions in a saucepan. Add the abalone and simmer over a gentle heat for 1 ½ hours. Turn off the heat and allow the abalone to cool in the stock. Slice into strips.

Soak the black moss in water for 10 minutes, then drain and lightly squeeze to remove excess moisture.

Combine the sugar, cornflour and water, stirring until smooth.

Heat the wok with the reserved oil and briefly scald the celtuce. Scoop out of the oil, leaving some oil in the wok, and spread on a serving platter.

Fry the remaining spring onions in the wok until fragrant, then scoop out of the oil. Discard oil. Add the abalone, oyster and soy sauces and lower the heat. Simmer gently for 10 minutes, then scoop out the abalone pieces and lay them over the celtuce.

Stir the cornflour mixture into the sauce. Add the black moss and simmer for a couple of minutes.

Come and get it
Spoon the black moss and sauce onto the abalone and celtuce and serve. Garnish with the spring onions.

SQUID, OCTOPUS, URCHINS, CUCUMBERS AND SEA BIRDS

Winter squid stew

This hearty stew is a great winter warmer on nights when an Antarctic breeze is blowing up from the Southern Ocean. It's delicious spooned over a bowl of brown rice. The Chinese mustard greens are sold in Asian supermarkets; they're known as *gai choy*, look like large bok choy, and have a lovely peppery flavour.

2 medium squid (combined weight of around 1 kg/2lb 3 oz)
1 tablespoon light (unroasted) sesame oil or peanut oil
1 onion, chopped
3 cm (1 in) ginger, finely chopped
1 tablespoon shoyu soy sauce
1 tablespoon maltose
⅓ bunch Chinese mustard greens, leaves separated
1 teaspoon kudzu (see Glossary, page 248), dissolved in ¼ cup water
brown or white steamed rice

Pull the tentacles of the squid away from their bodies—the innards will come too. Cut below the eyes, discarding the head and innards. Pop out the beak from between the tentacles and discard. Draw out the strip of transparent cartilage from inside the bodies and discard. Insert a knife into the bodies and cut through the flesh to open out flat. Rinse the bodies and tentacles and pat dry. Cut the tentacles into 3 cm (1 in) pieces and the bodies into strips.

Heat the oil in a heavy-based saucepan and fry the onion until translucent. Add the ginger and squid and fry until the squid is opaque. Add the shoyu and 1 cup of water. Cover with a lid and simmer for 30 minutes.

Add the maltose and increase the heat to a fast simmer. Add the mustard greens and cook for 1 minute. Add the kudzu and stir until thick.

Come and get it
Serve on steamed rice.

Sea urchins with duck eggs 'à la coque'

Sea urchins are very popular in France and Spain. They have a wonderful soft flavour reminiscent of the sea. Open up the black, spiky creature with a pair of scissors or a knife and you will find their delicious orange roe inside. You can eat the roe raw or use it in sauces, omelettes or sushi, or simply mashed with butter and spread on a fillet of steamed fish, or even on toast!

The French phrase à la coque usually refers to eggs and means soft-boiled, although in this recipe the eggs are cracked into the hollowed urchin shells and baked in the oven to give the same result— runny yolks perfect for dipping toast soldiers into. The urchin roe mixed with butter adds another splendid dimension to the rich duck egg. This is a great starter to a seafood meal.

12 sea urchins
80 g (3 oz) salted butter, softened
6 fresh duck eggs
flaky salt and cracked pepper
ciabatta sourdough

Preheat the oven to 240°C (460°F).

Grab hold of one of the sea urchins with your hand inside a tea towel and locate its mouth on top. Insert a pair of scissors into it and carefully cut off the top third of the urchin shell. Scoop out the roe with a teaspoon and set aside. Repeat with the remaining urchins. Select six of the best-looking urchin shells and reserve.

Mix the roe with the softened butter. Break an egg into each of the urchin shells and season with salt and pepper. Top with a dollop of the butter. Place the urchin shells upright on a baking tray and bake for 8–10 minutes, until the egg whites are cooked but the yolks are still runny.

Come and get it
Serve with toasted ciabatta sourdough cut into soldiers or strips for dipping into the egg.

Betsey Broughton and the Burning of the Boyd

In the National Library in Canberra, there hangs a portrait of a little seven-year-old girl that was painted by the convict artist Richard Read in 1814. In the 1920s, the New Zealand–born art collector Rex Nan Kivell spotted the portrait in an antique shop in Salisbury, England. He instinctively thought something was curious about the work: the lighting was from Australia or New Zealand, not England. And so he purchased it, and, on closer inspection, found a manuscript tucked in the frame that told the most extraordinary tale of the events that led to its painting.

William Broughton, the free servant of Surgeon-General John White, arrived at Port Jackson aboard the *Sirius* on the First Fleet in 1788. Between 1792 and 1807 he had five children with Elizabeth Heatherton (alias Ann Glossop), who had arrived in 1792 aboard the *Pitt* after being sentenced to seven years' transportation. On 8 November 1809, Elizabeth sailed for England aboard the *General Boyd*. She took her two-year-old daughter, Betsey, and left the older children in the care of their father. Captain John Thompson charted a course to Whangaroa, on the North Island of New Zealand, where he planned to take on board a load of kauri spars, adding to his existing cargo of seal skins, whale oil and timber planks. On board, working his passage across the Tasman, was a Maori *rangatira* (hereditary chieftain), Te Ara, who was nicknamed George. For reasons that are now unclear, Thompson had Te Ara flogged three times during the passage. Once ashore, Te Ara showed the welts on his back to his brother Te Puhi and his father, Piopio. *Utu* (Maori retributive justice) was inevitable.

According to some accounts, the day after their arrival at Whangaroa, Te Puhi offered to show Thompson suitable stands of kauri, so the following day the captain and his party set out in two of the ship's boats. Once ashore and out of sight, they were set upon and clubbed to death. The Maori waited until the cover of darkness, and then dressed in their victims' clothing and paddled back out to the *Boyd*, which lay quietly at anchor. They climbed aboard and carried out a swift and decisive assault. Those below decks were called up and butchered. Five managed to hide in the rigging, looking down in horror at the carnage on the decks, as the attackers dismembered the bodies ready to be taken ashore and eaten. Those survivors were bludgeoned the following morning.

Around seventy of the ship's complement were killed. Ann Morley and her infant were found hiding in a cabin and spared. The club-footed cabin boy Thomas Davis also survived; some say the Maori took him to be the son of a devil. The second mate amused the Maori by making fish-hooks for them, but was slaughtered a couple of weeks later when his usefulness ran out. Little Betsey Broughton, whose mother was killed, was taken in by one of the chiefs.

News of the massacre filtered through to the Bay of Islands, where the *City of Edinburgh* was taking on cargo. Alexander Berry, the ship's supercargo, immediately made for Whangaroa to rescue any survivors. Part of Berry's own account reads:

> I ... inquired of the chiefs if there were any survivors, to which they readily replied in the affirmative mentioning their names with great familiarity, and even with an appearance of kindness and sympathy. They were informed that we had come to Wangeroa for the purpose of delivering the captives. I then pointed to my men and their muskets on one hand, and to a heap of axes on the other, bidding them take their choice, and either deliver the captives peaceably when they would be

paid for their ransom, or I would attack them. The chief, after a moment's hesitation, replied with great quickness that trading was better than fighting, then give us your axes and you shall have your prisoners.

On being told that the captives were 'up the country, that they would immediately send for them and that they would be delivered up early next morning', the rescue party spent the night on an island—a 'small perpendicular rock' near the wreck of the *Boyd*, which was clearly easy to defend.

Next morning the natives, agreeable to promise, brought to our quarters a young woman and her sucking child and a boy belonging to the vessel, about fifteen years old.

On inquiring of the female whether there were any other survivors, she mentioned the infant daughter of Mr. Commissary Broughton, with whose family I was intimately acquainted. I thereupon applied to the chief demanding of its restitution ... He replied that it was in the possession of the chief of the island at the entrance of the harbour.

So the child who was Betsey Broughton was eventually delivered up,

tolerably clean, with its hair dressed and ornamented with white feathers, in the fashion of New Zealand. Its only clothing, however, consisted of a linen shirt which from the marks upon it, had belonged to the Captain ... When brought to the boat it cried out in a feeble and complaining tone, 'Mamma, my Mamma!'

The four survivors were taken by Berry on board the *City of Edinburgh* as passengers, and the ship left the Bay of Islands later in January 1810. Berry entrusted the two orphaned girls to the care of the Spanish family of Don Gasperde de Rico for eleven months, while Berry sailed back to England. In Rio de Janeiro, he met up with the captain of the British brig *Atlanta*, who was headed for Sydney and who agreed to return the children to their fathers. They arrived back in Australia in May 1812. In 1814, when Betsey was aged seven, William Broughton commissioned the convict artist Richard Read to paint her portrait, to be sent to Don Gasperde de Rico and his family in gratitude for the care they had given Betsey. The story of how the painting eventually made it into the antique shop in Salisbury is lost in the mists of time.

Costa Rican rice with baby octopus

2 cups rice
3 cloves
2 cinnamon sticks
3 cardamom pods
¼ cup light-flavoured oil such as grapeseed
2 large onions, chopped
4 garlic cloves, 2 crushed, 2 smashed with the skin on
1 tablespoon coriander seeds
6 baby octopus
1 tablespoon tomato paste
1 cup coriander (cilantro) leaves
½ cup lime juice
salt and pepper

Place the rice in a saucepan and add the cloves, cinnamon, cardamom and 3 cups of water. Bring to the boil with the lid on, then simmer very gently for 20 minutes.

Meanwhile, heat two-thirds of the oil in a frying pan and add the onion, crushed garlic and coriander seeds, frying until the onion starts to soften.

In another frying pan, heat the remaining oil and fry the smashed garlic until aromatic. Add the octopus and sear on all sides, then add the tomato paste. Mix with the onion, then add the coriander leaves and leave to stand for 30 minutes.

Come and get it
Combine the rice with the octopus and onion mixture and lime juice and season with salt and pepper.

Squid in sambal tumis

This dish is hot, hot, hot, incorporating a fried chilli sambal (tumis means fried). After a month of fasting for Ramadan, Malay Muslims celebrate Hari Raya Idul Fitri, the festival of breaking the fast, with a great nosh-up. This is one of the dishes enjoyed during the feasting.

whole squid weighing around 700 g (1 lb 9 oz)
⅓ cup tamarind pulp
2 onions, chopped
10 small red chillies, seeded and chopped
2 tablespoons shrimp paste
½ cup peanut oil
¼ cup sugar
1 teaspoon salt
steamed rice

Pull the tentacles of the squid away from the body—the innards will come too. Cut below the eyes, discarding the head and innards. Pop out the beak from between the tentacles and discard. Draw out the strip of transparent cartilage from inside the body and discard. Insert a knife into the body and cut through the flesh to open out flat. Rinse the body and tentacles and pat dry. Cut the tentacles into 3 cm (1 in) pieces and the body into strips.

Combine the tamarind pulp with 1 cup of hot water, stirring to break up and dissolve the tamarind. Leave for 5 minutes, then strain out the solids.

Pound the onion, chilli and shrimp paste to a rough paste in a mortar.

Heat the oil in a wok and fry the onion paste until thick and fragrant. Add the tamarind water, sugar, salt and squid and cook for a few minutes. The oil should have risen to the surface.

Come and get it
Serve with steamed rice.

Galician-style octopus (*Pulpo á feira*)

This tapas dish originated in Galicia although is now popular throughout Spain. It's dead-simple to prepare, and the flavours are surprisingly complex. While the waxy kipfler potatoes are Dutch, not Spanish, they go perfectly with the dish. It is worth freezing and thawing the octopus first to help tenderise it.

1 bay leaf
tentacles of 1 large octopus (weighing around 1.5 kg/3 lb 5 oz)
500 g (1 lb 2 oz) kipfler potatoes, peeled
2 tablespoons hot paprika
flaky salt
2 tablespoons chopped flat-leaf parsley
1 cup extra-virgin olive oil

Fill a large pot with water, add the bay leaf and bring it to the boil. Attach a sturdy hook to the middle of the octopus tentacles and lower into the water for 15–20 seconds. Remove the octopus and wait for the water to boil again. Repeat this process 3 or 4 times to tenderise the octopus.

Leave the octopus in the water, add the potatoes and simmer gently until the potatoes are soft (about 30 minutes). At this stage, check if the octopus is tender by inserting a skewer into the thickest part of a tentacle. It should go in with slight resistance and come out easily. If the octopus is not yet tender, scoop the potatoes out with a slotted spoon and continue simmering the octopus. When ready, drain the octopus and slice into bite-sized discs.

Come and get it
Place the octopus on a large plate (traditionally a wooden one) and surround it with the potatoes. Sprinkle with the paprika, salt and parsley and drizzle with the olive oil. Serve warm with toothpicks alongside, and with a good, gutsy red wine.

Salt and pepper squid

There are endless permutations of this dish in restaurants, bars and even fish and chip shops. The secret is a very light batter, fresh or fresh-frozen squid, and only 1–2 minutes of cooking time in very hot, clean oil. Follow these guidelines and the dish will be delicious.

2 medium squid (combined weight of around 1 kg/2lb 3 oz)
1 baby cos (romaine) lettuce, leaves separated and halved
½ long cucumber, peeled, seeded and diced
1 lemongrass stalk, finely sliced
2 limes, cut into thin wedges
small red chillies to taste, finely sliced on the diagonal
handful of coriander (cilantro) sprigs
1 tablespoon black peppercorns
1 tablespoon Sichuan peppercorns
1 teaspoon salt
1 teaspoon Chinese five-spice
1 litre (2 pints) peanut oil
1 cup plain (all-purpose) flour
1 cup cornflour (cornstarch)
325 ml (12 fl oz) chilled soda water

Pull the tentacles of the squid away from their bodies—the innards will come too. Cut below the eyes, discarding the head and innards. Pop out the beak from between the tentacles and discard. Draw out the strip of transparent cartilage from inside the bodies and discard. Insert a knife into the bodies and cut through the flesh to open out flat. Rinse the bodies and tentacles and pat dry. Cut the tentacles in half. Score the surface of the bodies in a crisscross pattern and cut into strips.

Combine the cos lettuce, cucumber, lemongrass, lime, chilli and coriander in a large bowl.

Put the black peppercorns, Sichuan peppercorns and salt in a wok. Heat gently, stirring every so often, until the mixture is fragrant and the salt browns slightly. Remove from the heat and allow to cool, then grind in a mortar. Add the five-spice.

Heat the oil in the wok to 180°C (350°F). Meanwhile, combine the pepper mixture and flours in a mixing bowl, stirring well. Quickly whisk in the soda water, being careful not to over-mix the batter (a few lumps won't matter).

Dip the squid pieces lightly in the batter and shake off any excess. Drop into the hot oil and deep-fry in small batches for 1–2 minutes, until golden. Drain on a wire rack.

Come and get it
Toss the squid with the salad and serve immediately.

Braised sea cucumber with vegetables

The sea cucumber was Australia's major item of international trade prior to the arrival of Europeans. Macassans from the island of Celebes (Sulawesi) came south on monsoonal winds in their wooden proas and established semi-permanent settlements on the north coast of Australia to fish for the sea cucumber, also known as the sea slug, trepang or bêche-de-mer. This curious holothurian is esteemed by the Chinese as an aphrodisiac. It has a very mild yet distinct flavour, and like gnocchi or dumplings, takes up sauces and flavours readily. The sea cucumber is a culinary curiosity and this traditional Chinese recipe is a great introduction to it. You can buy frozen sea cucumber in Asian supermarkets.

3 frozen sea cucumbers, thawed
100 ml (3 ½ fl oz) peanut oil
9 thin slices of ginger, 6 cut into fine julienne
9 spring onions (scallions), finely chopped
1 tablespoon cornflour (cornstarch)
1 tablespoon sesame oil
6 dried shiitake mushrooms, softened in warm water and
    squeezed dry, stems discarded
1 carrot, julienned
²/₃ cup tinned bamboo strips
¾ cup chicken stock
¼ cup soy sauce
1 tablespoon rice wine
12 snow peas
steamed rice

Cut each sea cucumber in half lengthwise, with a spoon remove the gut, then slice diagonally into bite-sized pieces.

Heat 2 tablespoons of the peanut oil in wok and fry the sliced ginger and a third of the spring onions until fragrant. Add 2 cups of water and bring to the boil. Add the sea cucumber and cook for 3 minutes, then drain off the liquid and set the sea cucumbers aside.

Mix the cornflour, sesame oil and ⅓ cup of water in a cup. Heat the remaining peanut oil in the wok and add the julienned ginger and remaining spring onions and stir-fry until fragrant. Add the sea cucumber, shiitake mushrooms, carrot and bamboo and stir-fry until piping hot. Add the chicken stock, soy sauce and rice wine and cook for 10 minutes, or until the liquid has reduced by a third to a half.

Add the snow peas and toss until the pods are bright green. Add the cornflour mixture and stir quickly until thick and glossy.

Come and get it
Serve on steamed rice.

Jellyfish salad with chicken and daikon

This salad is refreshing on a summer's day. The jellyfish has a slightly crunchy texture and a very subtle but specific flavour.

250 g (9 oz) dried jellyfish
500 g (1 lb 2 oz) daikon, finely julienned
2 teaspoons salt
1 chicken breast, finely sliced
1 egg white
1 teaspoon cornflour (cornstarch)
1 teaspoon sesame oil, plus 2 tablespoons extra
4 dried shiitake mushrooms, softened in warm water and
    squeezed dry, stems discarded
2 tablespoons sugar
2 tablespoons mirin
¼ cup peanut oil
4 spring onions (scallions), cut into 2 cm (¾ in) pieces

Soak the jellyfish in cold water overnight. Rinse it the following morning and soak it in fresh water for the rest of the day, rinsing a couple of times.

Drain the jellyfish and soak it in boiling water for 15 minutes until soft.

Meanwhile, place the daikon in a mixing bowl and toss with the salt. After 5 minutes, squeeze the excess moisture from the daikon.

Drain the jellyfish and refresh well in cold water. Cut it into thin shreds and add to the daikon.

Combine the chicken with the egg white, cornflour and 1 teaspoon of sesame oil.

Heat 1 litre (2 pints) of water in a saucepan and add the shiitake mushrooms. Cook for 5 minutes then remove with a slotted spoon. Add the chicken, lower the heat and simmer until cooked, stirring to separate the pieces. Drain the chicken and rinse in cold water. Finely slice the shiitake and add to the daikon and jellyfish together with the chicken.

Dissolve the sugar in the mirin. Heat the peanut oil in a wok and stir-fry the spring onions until beginning to wilt. Add the mirin and 2 tablespoons of sesame oil and stir briefly. Add the spring onion dressing to the jellyfish.

Come and get it
Toss the salad and serve.

Pandora's Box

In early November 1790, the British Admiralty dispatched the frigate *Pandora* to the South Seas under Captain Edward Edwards to hunt down the *Bounty* mutineers and if possible recapture the *Bounty* and return her to England.

On board as third lieutenant was Thomas Hayward, who had sailed with Bligh in the *Bounty*'s launch after the mutiny, and the horrors of that trip would have been fresh in his mind. In March 1791, the *Pandora* glided into Matavai Bay's clear blue water, bringing vengeance and justice to paradise. Some of the mutineers were overjoyed to finally be going home; among the men on board were loyalists. Others escaped into the hills only to be rounded up and brought on board the *Pandora*.

For three months, Edwards sailed about the Pacific in a fruitless search for the *Bounty*. With his new passengers, he did not distinguish between innocence and guilt: he would leave that to the court martial back in England. All fourteen were clapped in irons. The ship's carpenters set about building a suitable enclosure for the prisoners on the quarterdeck—a wooden box measuring 18 feet by 11 feet with just two narrow scuttles to allow in air. At first Edwards permitted the captives' Tahitian wives and children aboard. Ship's surgeon George Hamilton wrote: 'The prisoners' Tahitian wives visited the ship daily and brought their children to their unhappy fathers. To see the poor captives in irons, weeping over their tender offspring, was too moving a scene for any feeling heart'. Edwards soon stopped this, however, so the relatives waited in boats around the ship, screaming, wailing and cutting their heads until they drew blood. The prisoners were no longer allowed out of the box at all. They ate, slept and used 'necessary tubs' to answer the call of nature. The scene inside the box was nightmarish.

Eventually, Edwards turned for home and headed towards the Great Barrier Reef and Endeavour Strait— the route determined by the Admiralty that he should take. Approximately 85 miles east of Cape York, at 7.20 p.m. on 29 August 1791, the *Pandora* violently struck the Great Barrier Reef. Within five minutes there was 4 feet of water in the hold. While the reef was just submerged, the surrounding water was 100 feet deep.

In the darkness, the fourteen prisoners could only listen from their box to the disaster that was unfolding around them. Shortly after dawn, the armourer's mate removed their chains, but they were still locked in the box. The ship lurched over and began to sink. The prisoners begged the master-at-arms to leave the scuttle open, but he replied, 'Never fear my boys; we'll all go to hell together'. Through the hatch the prisoners could see the captain swimming for his pinnace. The box began to fill with water. At the last possible moment, William Moulter, the boatswain's mate, released the bolt and the prisoners scrambled out. Captain Edwards recorded, 'On mustering we discovered that 89 of the ship's company and 10 of the pirates were saved, and that 31 of the ship's company and 4 pirates were lost with the ship'.

For three days Edwards mustered his men and supplies on a small, unsheltered sandy cay about 3 miles from the wreck site. The prisoners were herded together at one end of the cay under armed guard, and were refused any shade. They had been months in the box, and their skin peeled off them in great lumps; they appeared to have been 'dipped in large tubs of boiling water'. To try to protect themselves from the tropical sun they buried themselves in the sand.

Edwards decided to repeat Bligh's 1000-mile run to Timor, this time in a flotilla of four small boats. One can only feel for poor Thomas Hayward, who, twice in as many years, had made the hot, dry, perilous and uncomfortable journey across the Arafura and Timor seas in an open boat. While the weather was kinder than it had been to Bligh, they were forced to drink the blood of birds and their own urine; however, they all survived. King George and Captain Bligh would see justice done.

Wendy's mutton-bird curry

The short-tailed shearwater or mutton-bird of south-eastern Australia is the most abundant native sea-bird species in all Australian waters. It is migratory, flying non-stop across the Pacific Ocean to Alaska's Aleutian Islands and Russia's Kamchatka Peninsula for the boreal summer each year.

In 1798, on his journey through Bass Strait, Matthew Flinders observed an incredible flock of mutton-birds and wrote of:

> a number of the sooty petrels as we had never seen equalled. There was a stream of from 50 to 80 yards in depth, and of 300 yards, or more, in breadth; the birds were not scattered, but flying as compactly as a free movement of their wings seemed to allow; and during a full hour and a half, this stream of petrels continued to pass without interruption, at a rate little inferior to the swiftness of the pigeon. Taking the stream to have been 50 yards deep by 300 in width, and that it moved at the rate of 30 miles an hour, and allowing 9 cubic yards of space to each bird, the number would amount to 151 500 000. The burrows required to lodge this quantity of birds would be 75 750 000; and allowing a square yard to each burrow, they would cover something more than 181 geographic square miles of ground.

Uncannily, almost the entire colony of short-tailed shearwaters will return to its nesting grounds on the same date in spring each year, with individuals returning to the same burrow. For a few weeks they will clean their burrows and then mate, and then the colony will disappear to sea for a couple of weeks. When they return, their eggs are laid: one single egg to each pair. The parents take turns to incubate the egg until it hatches, and two or three days afterwards the parents take to sea again for food. Every evening at dark the birds return from the sea, their agility astonishing as they silently swoop down to land right at their burrows.

The time the birds stay away lengthens, until in autumn the parents depart altogether, commencing their long journey back to the northern Pacific. Hunger soon sets in on the well-fed chicks—at this stage they usually weigh more than their parents—and incredibly, without any assistance, they take flight and find their own way north. In 1959 an Eskimo in the Bering Sea killed a fledgling that had been banded in Bass Strait. The bird had flown an incredible 15 000 kilometres in one month!

When the chicks fledge they weigh about 900 grams and this is usually when they are harvested from their burrows, a practice only allowed in Tasmania and limited to a strict time in autumn. Many of the burrows are shared by tiger snakes so the operation requires bravado.

This recipe comes from my good friend Wendy Jubb-Stoney. Wendy grew up on Flinders and Cape Barren islands and still returns regularly to her house there. I couldn't work out how to cook mutton-birds to mask their strong fishy flavour until she showed me. The secret is to render the oil thoroughly.

Wendy's mutton-bird curry (continued)

4 large red onions, chopped
3 cm (1 in) ginger, chopped
2 garlic cloves, chopped
small red chillies to taste, chopped
6 mutton-birds, cleaned
½ teaspoon turmeric
1 teaspoon ground cumin
1 teaspoon ground coriander
1 teaspoon garam masala
300 g (10 ½ oz) tinned tomatoes, chopped
225 g (8 oz) almond meal
salt and sugar to taste
steamed rice
coriander (cilantro) leaves
sultana and ginger chutney (page 184)

Combine the onions, ginger, garlic and chilli in a food processor and blend to a smooth paste.

Quarter each mutton-bird and trim off all visible fat.

Heat the fat in a frying pan and render it over medium-high heat (below the point of burning or being too smoky) until you have about half a cup of liquid fat. Brown the mutton-bird pieces in the fat.

Place the mutton-bird in an ovenproof dish that has a tight-fitting lid, leaving most of the fat in the pan. Add the onion paste to the pan and fry until aromatic. Add the turmeric, cumin, coriander and garam masala, stirring constantly. Add the tomatoes and cook until they dissolve into a sauce.

Meanwhile, preheat the oven to 180°C (350°F). Pour the sauce over the mutton-bird, put the lid on and bake for half an hour.

Remove from the oven and add the almond meal, stirring thoroughly. Season with salt and sugar if necessary. Bake for another few minutes. The flesh should have started to come away from the bones.

Come and get it
Serve on steamed rice garnished with coriander, and with sultana and ginger chutney on the side.

Squid-ink linguine with seafood

When squid are running under a jetty, one catches glimpses of silver streaks darting at impossible speeds through the water. When this happens, it is not unusual to bag your limit in no time; they often seem to jump right on your jig. It can be a messy business, especially when they deposit their ink all over you. Much better if you can put the ink to good use. The Renaissance masters used squid ink to create their beautiful sepia drawings; today it's most commonly used in cooking. In this recipe it colours homemade linguine, which contrasts beautifully against the seafood and parsley. If you are using fresh ink, you will find the thin, bluey-silver ink sac when you pull the tentacles away from the body, among the innards. Carefully cut it out.

Linguine
2 extra-large eggs
ink sacs from 4 squid or a packet of squid ink (available from Italian stores)
2 cups plain (all-purpose) flour
1 ½ tablespoons extra-virgin olive oil
salt

Seafood
½ cup extra-virgin olive oil
4 garlic cloves, roughly chopped
200 g (7 oz) prawn meat
200 g (7 oz) mussel meat
200 g (7 oz) calamari rings
200 g (7 oz) rockling, cut into bite-sized pieces
1 lemon, zested and juiced
1 cup roughly chopped flat-leaf parsley, plus extra sprigs to garnish
flaky salt and cracked pepper

Put the eggs and ink sacs in a food processor and pulse to combine.

Mound the flour on a work surface and make a well in the middle. Strain the egg and squid ink mixture into the well (to remove the sacs) and add the oil and a pinch of salt. Using a fork, mix the eggs and oil together, gradually incorporating the flour. Put the fork down and keep incorporating the flour with your hands until you have a smooth dough, aiming to use as much of the flour as possible. Set the dough aside and scrape the remaining flour from the bench into a bowl. Sift it back onto the bench, discarding any small pieces of dough. Return the dough to the flour, kneading for a couple of minutes to incorporate the flour.

Roll the dough through a pasta machine into thin sheets and cut into ribbons.

Bring a large pot of water to the boil over high heat. Add 2 tablespoons of salt and the pasta and stir to prevent it sticking together. Cook until al dente. My method for this is to put a lid on the pot and wait for the water to return to the boil. The moment it does, I cook the pasta for a further 15 seconds, then drain it. Keep the pasta warm while you cook the seafood.

Heat the oil in a large frying pan and sauté the garlic until fragrant. Add the seafood and toss until lightly cooked. Add the lemon zest and juice and stir briefly. Add the parsley and season with salt and pepper. Tip the linguine into the pan, turn off the heat and toss well.

Come and get it
Use tongs to place the pasta in bowls with a twisting motion, creating a nice swirl. Top with a selection of the cooked seafood and garnish with sprigs of parsley.

SAUCES, DIPS AND SIDES

Taramasalata

I love taramasalata on pita bread with fresh bean sprouts. It is a staple on the meze platter I have served on countless expeditions over the years, and a favourite lunch on the beach during summer holidays. Factory-made taramasalata does not compare. Give it a try—once you've been there, there is no going back.

100 g (3 ½ oz) tarama (Greek carp or cod roe) or salmon roe
2 medium potatoes, boiled and peeled
½ onion, grated
1 garlic clove, crushed
1 cup extra-virgin olive oil
2 lemons, juiced

Blend the roe and potatoes in a food processor at low speed. Add the onion and garlic and blend well.
    Slowly whisk the olive oil into the lemon juice in a bowl. Blend into the roe mixture. Store in a container in the refrigerator and use within a week or so.

Sultana and ginger chutney

3 cups sultanas
1 cup chopped ginger
2 small red chillies
1 teaspoon salt
1 lemon, juiced
¼ cup honey

Put the ingredients in a heavy-based saucepan and gently simmer until reduced to a dark paste (1 hour or so). Store in a jar in the refrigerator.

Nam pla prik

Nam pla prik—chilli fish sauce—is the dip I make whenever I am preparing a really quick fish or seafood meal at home. It takes no time at all and goes well with any fish or seafood.

¼ cup fish sauce
2 limes, juiced
2 garlic cloves, crushed
5 small green chillies, finely sliced
a few coriander (cilantro) leaves to garnish

Mix the ingredients in a bowl and scatter the coriander leaves on top.

Nam prik narok

The translation for this magnificent Thai dip is 'hell-hot chilli water', so consider yourself warned! Use as a dipping sauce or a paste to stir-fry prawns in.

2 cups peanut oil
1 kg (2 lb 3 oz) skinless, boneless soft white fish fillets such as rockling, diced
1 cup dried red chillies
8 garlic cloves, skin on
3 shallots, skin on
2 tablespoons shrimp paste
⅓ cup palm sugar
¼ cup fish sauce

Heat the oil in a wok until hot and fry the fish until golden brown and cooked through.

Char the chillies, garlic and shallots on a barbecue. Peel the skins from the garlic and shallots. Pound all to a smooth paste in a large mortar (or use a food processor), then add the fish and continue pounding until smooth.

Form the shrimp paste into a ball, skewer with a fork and toast over a flame on the stovetop until the colour has lightened and it has started smoking. (Or if your paste is too dry to form a ball, wrap it in foil.)

Combine the shrimp paste, palm sugar and fish sauce in a saucepan and heat, stirring until dissolved. Add to the fish paste and stir thoroughly.

Store in a jar in the refrigerator.

Guacamole

Guacamole was originally a food of the Aztecs, made by mashing avocados with tomatoes. The conquistadors brought it back to Europe. Guacamole is great with a simple fillet of fish or with prawns.

2 avocados
2 limes, juiced
2 spring onions (scallions), finely chopped
¼ cup coriander (cilantro) leaves
small green chillies to taste, finely chopped

Place the ingredients in a mortar and roughly mash.

Harissa

150 g (5 oz) dried red chillies
1 tablespoon coriander seeds
1 tablespoon cumin seeds
1 teaspoon caraway seeds
12 garlic cloves
½ cup extra-virgin olive oil

Soak the chillies in a bowl of water for 1 hour, then chop them.

Grind the coriander, cumin and caraway seeds in a mortar. Add the garlic and chillies and pound to a fine paste. Add the olive oil. Use immediately or store in a jar in the refrigerator.

Maître d'hôtel butter

Butters are very traditional, but can be excellent when you just want to grill or steam a piece of fish and not go to too much trouble.

125 g (4 oz) butter, softened
1 teaspoon chopped flat-leaf parsley
½ lemon, juiced

Place the butter in a bowl and beat with a fork. Incorporate the parsley and lemon juice. Place on a sheet of greaseproof paper and roll into a sausage inside the paper. Chill until solid. Slice into wheels as needed.

Anchovy butter

This butter is nice and strong; try it with barbecued fish.

120 g (4 oz) butter, softened
16 anchovies in oil, drained
4 garlic cloves
cracked pepper

Pound the ingredients in a mortar until creamy. Place on a sheet of greaseproof paper and roll into a sausage inside the paper. Chill until solid. Slice into wheels as needed.

The Adventures of the Tom Thumb

During the long journey from England to Sydney aboard the *Reliance*, midshipman Matthew Flinders befriended the 24-year-old ship's surgeon George Bass, and they regularly discussed the prospect of exploring the Australian coast together. Stored within the ship's cutter was Bass' own boat—a tiny dinghy with an 8-foot keel and a 5-foot beam, aptly named the *Tom Thumb*.

Shortly after their arrival in the colony, they met with Governor Hunter to seek permission to explore the Georges River in the *Tom Thumb*, and Hunter acquiesced. On 26 October 1795, Flinders, Bass and his boy servant William Martin sailed the *Tom Thumb* through Sydney Heads and southward along the rugged coast. The mouth of the Georges River was located and they sailed as far upstream as possible, then walked and waded a further 20 miles before turning round and returning to Sydney Cove. They had proved themselves, and their reports of fertile soil enticed Governor Hunter to take a look for himself a couple of years later, resulting in the founding of Bankstown.

Flinders and Bass' next adventure was in a new, larger *Tom Thumb*—a whole 12 feet in length! Accompanied once again by Martin, they set out from Sydney on 24 March 1796. On board they had provisions to last ten days, two muskets, ammunition, two pocket compasses, a watch and a rock for an anchor.

By daybreak they were beyond the Heads, but they became becalmed and had to row down the coast. The day was sultry, and they soon discovered that their water had gone bad from being stored in an old wine barrel. By evening, the current had swept them 20 miles further south than they had intended, and without safe harbour they spent an uncomfortable night getting what sleep they could on the floor of the boat.

The morning found them desperate for water and with no choice but to go ashore. There was no opportunity to beach the *Tom Thumb*, so Bass swam the empty barrel to shore. Shortly afterwards, a freak wave lifted the *Tom Thumb* and dumped her onto the beach as well, thoroughly drenching their equipment. The boat was put to sea immediately, but it took some time to ferry the provisions back on board, and it was late afternoon before they were under sail again, off the coast of today's Wollongong. Unable to find shelter they spent another chilly night in the boat, with Bass badly sunburnt and in considerable pain.

The following morning, a couple of Aboriginals appeared on the beach before them, and promised the explorers plenty of women (including, interestingly, two white women, presumably escaped from Sydney), together with ducks, fish and water. Desperate for water, Flinders and Bass invited them aboard, and the Indigenous pilots guided the *Tom Thumb* through the entrance to what is now known as Lake Illawarra. Flinders amused the Aboriginals gathered there by shaving their beards. Then they dried their soaked gunpowder in the sun and filled the barrel with fresh water.

More Aboriginals arrived, and as the day progressed the Europeans started to feel insecure. They pushed the boat out into the lagoon, but the Aboriginals tried to drag it back, four of them jumping aboard. Flinders loaded a musket and fired a shot. The natives dispersed. The *Tom Thumb* moved downstream, and eventually they rowed clear of the lake's entrance and back to where they had anchored the night before.

The next day they beat north against the east-coast current and in the late afternoon found shelter on a beach beneath some cliffs, where they spent the night comfortably on the sand, even though Bass' back was now one huge blister. The following morning they rowed north upon a calm sea, but as the day progressed a strong northerly prevented their progress and they pulled in below the cliffs for shelter and dropped anchor. In the early evening the wind rose a 'southerly buster' and they set upon the rising sea in a northerly direction. In the inky darkness their little boat was tossed in the backwash as thunder roared and lightning strobed about them.

THE "TOM THUMB."

For an hour they kept this up, until they realised that there were high breakers ahead and no cliffs behind them. A split-second decision had to be made, 'as our bark could not live ten minutes longer'. On coming to the extremity of the breakers, they brought the boat around into the wind, dropped the mast and sail, and immediately started rowing, pulling with all their might toward the reef. Within a few seconds they were in smooth waters. They found a beach and, grateful to be alive, named it Providential Cove, now known as Wattamolla, in Sydney's Royal National Park.

The following morning, under a fresh southerly breeze, the *Tom Thumb* headed back into open water, and by late morning was sailing through a mile-wide entrance to a bay they named Port Hacking, after the quartermaster on the First Fleet's HMS *Sirius*. They spent the day exploring the estuary. The next day a southerly wind carried them northward again and, not long after sunset, the *Tom Thumb* was secured once more in Port Jackson.

The two *Tom Thumb* journeys were significant not only as heroic endeavours; they also enabled Flinders to make a practical start in hydrography. His navigation was surprisingly accurate, despite his having only a pocket compass. His eye-sketch survey was taken to England, and in March 1799 was published. For so young a man this was a great achievement, and it brought him under the watchful eye of men of influence, including Sir Joseph Banks. The *Tom Thumb* achieved the status of almost a religious relic: a small section of its timber was cased in silver and given to the French captain Nicolas Baudin by the governor.

Sea-urchin butter

This is good with scallops, bugs and prawns.

4 sea urchins
100 g (3 ½ oz) butter, softened
½ teaspoon grated lemon zest
cracked pepper

Remove the roe from the urchins by finding their mouths on top, inserting a pair of scissors and cutting them open (protect your hands by holding the urchins inside a tea towel). Scoop out the orange contents and place in a mortar.

Pound the roe to a smooth paste with the other ingredients. Use soon after making.

Saffron crustacean butter

This is good with scallops, crabs, bugs or lobster. It is also delicious tossed through pasta.

pinch of saffron threads
2 ½ tablespoons extra-virgin olive oil
250 g (9 oz) raw shells from prawns, bugs or blue swimmer crabs
200 g (7 oz) butter
1 tablespoon lemon juice
flaky salt and cracked pepper

Soak the saffron in a little warm water.

Heat the olive oil in a frying pan and add the shells. Fry until a rich red colour.

Combine the saffron and its water, shells and oil, butter, lemon juice, salt and pepper in a food processor and blend until smooth and creamy. Push through a fine sieve onto a sheet of greaseproof paper and roll into a sausage inside the paper. Chill until solid. Slice into wheels and use within a few days.

Prawn butter

Toss this with steamed lobster meat or melt it over a fillet of fish.

100 g (3 ½ oz) prawn meat, cooked
100 g (3 ½ oz) butter, softened
squeeze of lemon juice
cracked pepper

Pound all the ingredients to a smooth paste in a mortar. Place on a sheet of greaseproof paper and roll into a sausage inside the paper. Chill until solid. Slice into wheels and use within a few days.

Mayonnaise

One of the first things you learn at chef school is how to make mayonnaise; how to whisk like mad to generate that magic emulsion. Fortunately, food processors have made it a whole lot easier. It's still probably a good idea to master the manual technique, but this is the mechanical version.

For garlic mayonnaise, add a crushed garlic clove at the end, or for rouille, a traditional accompaniment to bouillabaisse (page 4), add 2 crushed garlic cloves, 1 teaspoon of tomato paste, a pinch of cayenne and a pinch of saffron powder.

2 egg yolks (for a richer mayonnaise, use duck eggs)
¼ teaspoon Dijon mustard
2 teaspoons vinegar or
    2 tablespoons lemon juice
300 ml (10 fl oz) olive oil (not extra-virgin)
salt
ground white pepper

Place the yolks, mustard and half of the vinegar or lemon juice in a food processor and blend for 20–30 seconds. With the machine running, slowly pour in the oil in a constant stream until the mixture emulsifies. Turn off the machine, add the rest of the vinegar or lemon juice and season to taste with salt and pepper. Pulse briefly.

Tartare

Traditional tartare is a sauce of hardboiled egg yolks mixed with chives, spring onions (scallions), gherkins or capers, or a mixture of a few of these. This is the better-known version in Australia, without the hardboiled eggs and with mayonnaise.

1 quantity mayonnaise (page 191)
⅓ cup capers in brine, rinsed and finely chopped
2 tablespoons finely chopped sweet gherkins
2 tablespoons finely chopped flat-leaf parsley
2 tablespoons finely chopped shallots

Stir all the ingredients together.

Cocktail sauce

I confess … I love this sauce, especially on cold prawns, crab, lobster or fish and chips!

1 quantity mayonnaise (page 191)
⅔ cup tomato sauce
¼ cup cream
1 teaspoon Worcestershire sauce
dash of Tabasco sauce
1 tablespoon lemon juice
1 tablespoon finely chopped flat-leaf parsley
cracked pepper

Stir all the ingredients together.

Hollandaise

Hollandaise goes well with steamed or poached fish such as salmon in court bouillon (page 46).

1 tablespoon white-wine vinegar or tarragon vinegar
pinch of ground white pepper
3 egg yolks
150 g (5 oz) unsalted butter

Combine the vinegar, pepper and ¼ cup of water in a small saucepan and boil until reduced to 1 teaspoon. Watch carefully so you don't end up with a burnt pan.

Put the butter in a separate saucepan and gently heat to just boiling, without browning.

Put the egg yolks in a food processor and blend until smooth. With the machine running, slowly pour in the vinegar and butter in a constant stream until the mixture emulsifies.

Bearnaise

Make bearnaise in the same way as hollandaise, except add 3 finely chopped spring onions (scallions) to the vinegar and water. When you have reduced the mixture, strain it through a fine sieve and add 1 teaspoon of chopped tarragon and ½ teaspoon of chopped chervil. Proceed with the rest of the recipe. Bearnaise goes well with crumbed fish.

Arame salad

This salad is heady with the essence of the sea and goes well with any poached or steamed fish. The flavour reminds me of the smells beneath a jetty: the rocks coated with sea cabbage washed with crystal-clear water, and a faint fishy smell that is fresh and alive, not dead. If you are aiming for visuals, then the jet-black colour of the arame blends beautifully with a garnish of thinly sliced lime and red chilli.

handful of dried arame
4 limes, juiced
¼ cup rice vinegar
1 tablespoon fish sauce

Soak the arame in cold water until soft (about 5 minutes). Rinse well.

Bring a pot of water to the boil and cook the arame for 5–10 minutes. It will expand 4–5 times in size. Drain and refresh in a bowl of sea water or salted water for a few minutes. Drain again and rinse under fresh water.

Toss the arame with the lime juice, vinegar and fish sauce.

Wakame salad

This is great with Japanese fish dishes such as teriyaki yellowtail kingfish (page 62).

handful of dried wakame
1 long cucumber, peeled, seeded and cut into bite-sized chunks
2 tablespoons fine salt
⅓ cup brown-rice vinegar
flaky salt

Wash the wakame well and soak in cold water for 5 minutes. Drain and cut into bite-sized pieces.

Blanch the wakame in a saucepan of boiling water, then drain and refresh in iced water. Pat dry with paper towel.

Place the cucumber in a colander and toss with 2 tablespoons of salt. Leave for 10 minutes. Rinse off the salt and pat dry.

Combine the wakame, cucumber and vinegar in a bowl and season to taste with flaky salt.

Spicy wedges and rocket salad

This is a great way to jazz up a piece of grilled fish.

1 kg (2 lb 3 oz) potatoes
¼ cup Cajun spice
1 teaspoon Spanish smoked paprika
1 tablespoon cornflour (cornstarch)
1 teaspoon flaky salt
¼ cup extra-virgin olive oil
50 g (2 oz) wild rocket (arugula)
1 lemon, juiced

Cut the potatoes into thick wedges with the skin on. Soak in water for 30 minutes.

Preheat the oven to 200°C (400°F). Drain the wedges and pat them dry with a tea towel. Place in a plastic bag with the spices, cornflour and salt. Shake the bag to coat the wedges.

Pour the olive oil onto a baking tray and spread the wedges on top. Bake for 45 minutes, turning the wedges every 15 minutes, until crisp.

Combine the rocket and lemon juice in a large bowl. Toss through the hot wedges and serve immediately.

Tunisian orange, almond and date salad

This sweet and refreshing salad is a magnificent accompaniment to North African fish dishes (and it also makes a good dessert). The orange-blossom water gives an exotic dimension.

6 oranges
1 tablespoon orange-blossom water
8 fresh dates, pitted and finely julienned
100 g (3 ½ oz) slivered almonds, toasted
1 tablespoon mint leaves, finely shredded
¼ teaspoon ras el hanout spice mix (or substitute cinnamon)

Take off the peel and pith from the oranges with a knife. Cut out the segments by carefully slicing on the insides of the membranes. Place the segments in a bowl. Squeeze the juice out of the remaining membranes into the bowl. Add the orange-blossom water. Cover and chill in the refrigerator until ready to serve.

Place the orange segments on a plate and pour over the juice. Scatter the dates and almonds over the top and sprinkle with the mint and ras el hanout. Serve immediately.

DESSERTS

Campari granita

This is not overly sweet like some other desserts. It's more of a refreshing appetiser or palate cleanser to serve between courses on a hot summer's day.

⅓ cup campari
2 tablespooons caster sugar
1 ½ cups blood-orange juice
1 ½ cups orange juice

Mix the campari, sugar and juice and freeze in an ice-cream machine to the manufacturer's instructions. Otherwise, pour into a tray and place in the freezer. When almost frozen, pulse the mixture in a food processor, return to the tray and refreeze.

Come and get it
Scoop into glasses and serve.

Summer rockmelon agar

This is a great cooling dish for a hot day; very clean on the palate. It contains no sugar and the use of agar (as opposed to gelatine) makes it suitable for vegetarians. Agar is a sea vegetable that grows in tidal environments across the world, including Australia. In the Western District of Victoria, early settlers used to gather white agar flakes on the shorelines of beaches to make jelly. Agar can be purchased in bars, shredded in threads or in powder form. Unlike gelatine, it sets at room temperature.

1.25 litres (2 pints 10 fl oz) apple juice
1 cup agar threads
1 tablespoon arrowroot or kudzu (see Glossary, page 248),
    dissolved in ¼ cup water
1 rockmelon, skinned and seeded, ½ puréed and ½ diced in
    small cubes
1 lemon, juiced
2 tablespoons shredded mint

Bring the apple juice to the boil, then add the agar and stir until dissolved. Simmer for 10 minutes, stirring frequently. Add the arrowroot or kudzu and stir for 2 minutes. Remove from the heat and leave to cool for 5 minutes. Stir in the rockmelon purée, cubed rockmelon, lemon juice and mint. Pour into a mould and chill in the refrigerator for around 30 minutes.

Come and get it
Slice into portions and serve on flat plates or in bowls.

Fresh fruit with chilled chocolate pernod fondue

200 g (7 oz) dark chocolate
300 g (10 ½ oz) caster (superfine) sugar
1 cup pernod
strawberries
sliced banana

Melt the chocolate in a bowl set over a saucepan of simmering water.

Put the sugar and 2 cups of water in a separate saucepan and gently heat until the sugar dissolves. Raise the heat and boil for 1 minute. Gradually stir into the melted chocolate, then stir in the pernod. Blend in a food processor for a smooth consistency. Leave to cool to room temperature, then freeze for at least 1 hour (the alcohol content means the mixture won't actually freeze).

Come and get it

Arrange strawberries and banana on a platter with a bowl of the chilled chocolate sauce. Dip the fruit into the sauce.

Ginger tapioca

Ginger aficionados will love this dish—the smooth pearls of tapioca contrast wonderfully with the crunch of the crystallized ginger.

1 ½ cups tapioca
125 g (4 oz) ginger
1 cup sweetened condensed milk
2 tablespoons roughly chopped crystallised ginger

Fill a large saucepan with water and bring to the boil. Lower the heat and add the tapioca, stirring to prevent it sticking or clumping together. Simmer until almost transparent, with just a little spot of white left in the centre of the pearls. Drain and refresh under cold water. Place in a bowl.

Grate the ginger and squeeze the juice through muslin cloth, or extract in a juicer.

Warm the condensed milk in a saucepan. Add to the tapioca along with the ginger juice and roughly chopped crystallised ginger and stir well.

Come and get it
Scoop into parfait or long-stemmed glasses and serve.

Green tea and white chocolate pannacotta

The delightful flavour of the green tea makes this a complex flavoured exotic dessert. If you like, instead of pouring the mix into moulds, place it in an ice-cream maker for a wonderful ice-cream.

2 gelatine sheets
½ cup milk
1 tablespoon green-tea powder
½ cup coconut cream
1 cup cream
65 g (2 oz) caster (superfine) sugar
50 g (1 ¾ oz) white chocolate, chopped

Soften the gelatine in a bowl of cold water.

Put 2 tablespoons of the milk in a saucepan and stir in the green-tea powder. Squeeze the excess water from the gelatine and add to the milk along with all remaining ingredients. Bring to a gentle simmer, stirring until the gelatine and white chocolate dissolve. Pour into moulds or glasses (I use liqueur glasses) and refrigerate overnight covered with plastic wrap.

Come and get it
Serve chilled.

Calvados apple cake

Calvados is a French brandy made from apples. If you can't get hold of it, use brandy, cognac or Armagnac.

300 g (10 ½ oz) caster (superfine) sugar
6 Granny Smith apples, peeled and cored, cut into eighths
⅓ cup calvados
120 g (4 oz) butter
2 eggs
1 cup self-raising flour, sifted

Butter a cake tin (I use a fluted ring tin).

Put two-thirds of the sugar in a heavy-based frying pan and slowly melt over low–moderate heat for 6–8 minutes, only stirring at the edges as they begin to caramelise. Add the apples and calvados. Continue to cook for a further 6–8 minutes, turning the apples carefully, until caramelised and cooked through. Tip into the base of the cake tin.

Preheat the oven to 180°C (350°F). Cream the butter with the remaining sugar until light and fluffy. Add the eggs one at a time, beating well after each addition. Gently fold in the flour. Spread the mixture over the apples and bake for 45 minutes, or until a skewer inserted into the cake comes out clean.

Come and get it
Leave the cake to cool in the tin for 10 minutes or so before inverting onto a plate.

Lost at Sea
The Sydney to Hobart Yacht Race 1998

The Sydney to Hobart Yacht Race is an institution in Australian sport, ranking alongside iconic events like the Melbourne Cup, the AFL grand finals and, on the same day, the venerable Boxing Day Test at the Melbourne Cricket Ground. Hosted by the Cruising Yacht Club of Australia and run in cooperation with the Royal Yacht Club of Tasmania, the race is approximately 630 nautical miles. First held in 1945, initially planned to be a cruise, the event has grown over the decades to become one of the pre-eminent offshore yacht races in the world, and now attracts maxi-yachts from around the globe, many carrying corporate sponsorship to help offset the massive expenditure required to compete. Some commentators describe it as the 'Everest of the Sea'.

Bass Strait and the waters of the Tasman Sea immediately to its east are renowned for their high winds and difficult seas. Even though the race is held in the Australian summer, 'southerly buster' storms often make the journey cold, rough and very challenging for the crews. It is typical for a reasonable portion of the flotilla to retire without staying the course, often retreating into the port of Eden on the New South Wales South Coast, the last safe harbour before the Bass Strait crossing. Those who make the crossing sail down the rocky east coast of Tasmania to round the Tasman Peninsula into Storm Bay and cross the finish line off Battery Point in the wide Derwent River. Traditionally, the crews of the yachts celebrate New Year's Eve at Constitution Dock in Hobart, partying hard into the night.

On Boxing Day 1998, there were 115 boats jostling to cross the start line. It was a brilliant, bright summer day, and the pennants and ensigns on the flotilla of small craft filled with thousands of sightseers created a sea of colour as the armada of blue water yachts cleared the Sydney Heads and raised their spinnakers for the run south. They didn't realise that the warm air filling their sails was going to collide with cold air blowing up from the Southern Ocean, resulting in a great storm. They were racing headlong towards a cell that would produce winds of up to 90 miles per hour and whip the seas to an average height of 65 feet, with freak waves in excess of 90 feet. Not even the Bureau of Meteorology comprehended the magnitude of the system. Local fisherman on the south coast had sniffed the breeze and were either scampering back to port or preparing to 'stooge'—hove to and ride it out.

Early on 27 December, helicopter pilot Ray Stone said goodbye to his wife and two kids on their farm at Elizabeth Hill and drove to Canberra Airport, to commence a three-day shift flying the Bell 412 rescue helicopter, call-sign Southcare 1. It was a blustery morning with hot winds from the west and an angry sky. His crew for the day were Mark Delf, a navy veteran of twenty years, and two young female paramedics, Michelle Blewitt and Kristy McAlister.

They received instructions to head to a point 65 nautical miles off the coast at Merimbula, where Helimed 1, another of the company's helicopters, was already pulling survivors from the boat *Offshore Stand Aside*. Southcare 1 cleared the coast and flew out into a perfect storm. Beneath it was a maelstrom of eight-storey-high waves. The blue-black cloud base was just 300 feet above, and the wind was howling at 75 miles per hour. They finally located the landing light of Helimed 1. Holding orbit at 200 feet, they watched as the Helimed's rescue paramedic was lowered into the violent sea and dragged 160 feet over to the stern of the boat, where sailors were abandoning ship into a life-raft. When Helimed 1 pulled away to return to Mallacoota with eight survivors, it was time for Southcare 1 to move in and pick up the rest. Ray had to fly without visual cues, dependent on constant dialogue from Mark to enable him to position the aircraft. The best description of what happened next is Ray's own:

Mark Delf and the two paramedics spent the next half hour extracting the four remaining yachties as the weather and dark rolled in. By the end of it they were totally exhausted.

Our 'customers' were repeatedly thrown out of the life-raft (the yachties were hopping into the raft from the dismasted, un-roofed yacht) and had to be chased through the maelstrom.

Kristy (first into the water—she did two and then Michelle did two) was rolled by a huge wave (I had to lift the helicopter to get out of its way) and came up with the winch cable wrapped around her neck—a recipe for instant decapitation.

The raft got blown over onto Michelle and the metre-long CO_2 cylinder hit her in the head. If she hadn't been wearing her flying helmet she would have been brained. The raft's tether fouled the winch cable; a gust picked up the raft, pulled the cable to full extension and wrenched my crewman out of the helicopter. He was harnessed to the helicopter, of course, but Kristy, who had already been 'down the wire' twice herself, had to pull him back inside.

All I knew of the event was Mark firmly calling 'Move right ... move right ... move right!' ... I moved right. Michelle, in the water, was fighting a terrified survivor and trying to untangle the line. In the end she cut the raft away and thereby removed a serious impediment to the rescue—the raft was an utter liability from start to finish!

The skipper was the last off the boat—he tied a line to himself and jumped, swam clear, and we picked him up in about five minutes flat.

We hacked back through the tempest at 100 feet to get out of the headwind and landed at Mallacoota just on dark. The tired, wet, freezing paramedics were philosophical about the whole thing. Michelle made the observation that—'I'm never f—ing getting on another f—ing helicopter again as long as I f—ing live'.

At 7 a.m. the next morning, both Michelle and Kristy stepped up to board the 'bug-smasher' flight to Merimbula, to recommence the rescue. For the next three days, as the storm passed and the seas gradually abated, they flew endless search patterns way out to sea in search of missing sailors. They found nothing but the drifting hulk of the *Business Poste-Naiad* with a deceased sailor lying serenely in the cockpit, and a half-inflated life-raft 80 miles out to sea, where they were searching for the missing crew of the *Winston Churchill*.

In the 1998 Sydney to Hobart, twenty-four boats were crushed and abandoned, fifty-seven sailors were rescued, and six men died. On 12 December 2000, two weeks before the start of that year's race, New South Wales coroner John Abernethy handed down his findings on the 1998 race deaths, saying that the Cruising Yacht Club of Australia had 'abdicated its responsibility to manage the race'. He was also highly critical of the Australian Bureau of Meteorology. Each crewmember of Southcare 1 later received the American Helicopter Society William J Kosser Award, the Leith Award (Scotland), Australian bravery decorations and the Bravery Cross from the Royal Lifesaving Society of Australia.

Black sticky rice (*kao niow dahm*) with mango

This Thai masterpiece is a favourite. The nutty flavour of the black rice—really a deep red—combined with the coconut and sugar will keep you coming back for more. Black rice from Indonesia or Thailand is usually the best.

400 g (14 oz) black glutinous rice, soaked overnight
1 cup coconut cream
150 g (5 oz) sugar
1 teaspoon salt
1 pandan leaf, tied in a knot
3 mangos, cheeks scored
mint leaves
fried shallots

Rinse the soaked rice in cold water to remove excess starch. Put in a bowl that will allow one-third expansion. Barely cover with hot water and place in a bamboo steamer set over a wok of boiling water. Steam for 30–40 minutes, until tender.

Meanwhile, combine the coconut cream, sugar, salt and pandan leaf in a saucepan and heat until the sugar dissolves. Stir half into the rice. Leave to stand for 15 minutes.

Come and get it
Scoop the rice into small bowls, gently flattening it down, then invert onto plates. Slice off cubes of mango from the scored cheeks and place beside the rice. Drizzle the remaining coconut cream over the top. Garnish with mint and fried shallots.

Pandan pannacotta

I like to top this pannacotta with coconut jelly and palm seeds. You can buy cubed coconut jelly in jars and palm seeds in tins (both are in syrup) from most Asian supermarkets.

2 ½ leaves gelatine
100 ml (3 ½ fl oz) milk
560 ml (19 fl oz) cream
100 g (3 ½ oz) caster (superfine) sugar
¼ teaspoon pandan paste
coconut jelly cubes
palm seeds

Soften the gelatine in a bowl of cold water.

Gently heat the milk in a small saucepan until almost boiling. Squeeze the excess water from the gelatine and stir into the milk.

Heat the cream and sugar in a separate saucepan, stirring until the sugar dissolves. Remove from the heat and stir in the pandan paste. Stir in the milk, then pour into moulds or glasses (I use liqueur glasses) and refrigerate until set.

Come and get it
Top with coconut jelly and palm seeds and serve.

Roast apricots with abbamele

Abbamele is an ancient honey product of Sardinia. After honey has been collected, leftover honey and pollen is extracted and reduced and often flavoured with citrus. I like to make a kind of abbamele by simmering honey with orange and lemon zest and adding juice at the end.

Apricots
1 cup brown sugar, plus 1 tablespoon extra
1 teaspoon ground cardamom
12 apricots, halved and stoned
2 tablespoons butter

Abbamele
1 orange
1 lemon
1 cup honey

good vanilla ice-cream

Preheat the oven to 180°C (350°F). Mix 1 cup of brown sugar with the cardamom in a bowl and toss through the apricot halves to coat them. Lay them on a lightly buttered baking tray cut-side up. Place a little of the butter in each cavity and roast for 15 minutes or until soft. Sprinkle the extra sugar over the apricots, increase the oven temperature to 200°C (400°F) and roast for a further 5 minutes, or until the apricots caramelise.

For the abbamele, cut off two strips of rind from both the orange and lemon and juice to give ¼ cup each. Put the honey and rind in a heavy-based saucepan and gently bring to the boil. Reduce the heat and simmer for 30 minutes. Remove the rind and stir in the juice.

Come and get it
Place the apricots in bowls, drizzle the warm abbamele over the top and serve with scoops of vanilla ice-cream.

Matthew Flinders

Shipwrecked!

When Matthew Flinders returned to Port Jackson in June 1803 after his great circumnavigation of Terra Australis, his worm-ridden ship *Investigator* was condemned. As there were no other ships available in the colony for Flinders to complete his surveys, Governor Philip Gidley King decided he should return to England to obtain another vessel from the Admiralty.

Flinders sailed on the HMS *Porpoise* on 10 August under the command of Lieutenant Fowler and accompanied by twenty-one of his former crew and the artist William Westall. He sailed as a passenger so he could devote all of his time to completing his charts for the Admiralty. Two East Indiamen accompanied them, the *Cato* and the *Bridgewater*, bound for Batavia. Fowler was instructed to sail whichever route Flinders decided, and never to miss an opportunity. The young navigator requested they plot a course through the Torres Strait to double-check that the passage he had previously found was indeed safe. It was also the quickest route at that time of year.

Seven days later, 1900 kilometres out of Sydney, at 9.30 p.m. the cry went up from the watch on the *Porpoise*, 'Breakers ahead!' Fowler immediately gave the order to bring the ship about, but, with only double-reefed topsails set, she would not come around. Flinders, who had been working below, went on deck to see, in the darkness, the ghostly white of huge breakers crashing to leeward and the ship swinging away from the wind. After a few moments the *Porpoise* violently struck the reef. Unable to fire a gun or send up a light to warn the other ships, the crew watched helplessly as the *Cato* hit the reef and rolled onto her broadside, her masts disappearing in the darkness. The *Bridgewater* was the only ship left afloat, alone in the darkness amid a maze of reefs.

After hurriedly rescuing what he could of his precious charts, Flinders swam to a dinghy and attempted to row to the *Bridgewater* to make arrangements for the rescue of the stricken seamen. The boat leaked so badly that he had to bail with whatever came to hand, first the cook's boots, then one of the men's hats. It being unsafe to cross the breakers in darkness, he had to wait until dawn. One can only imagine his horror as he watched the lights of the *Bridgewater* recede into the inky darkness and disappear.

Flinders took command. Beyond the reef and the two stricken ships lay a sandbank, so he ordered the surviving crew to abandon the wrecks and swim through the breakers to shore. Three died; the rest of the company were saved. Rudimentary tents were constructed from torn sails, clothing was shared around and provisions landed. A flagstaff was constructed and an upside-down ensign run up to indicate distress. Naval discipline prevailed.

Flinders held a council that decided that the largest of the two six-oared cutters would be lightly decked over and that Flinders, together with Park, captain of the *Cato*, would proceed with a boat crew to Port Jackson to hire or obtain from Governor King enough vessels to carry everyone back to Sydney or on to India. Flinders believed he could return with salvation within two months. It was also decided that the remaining men would build two small boats and, in the event of Flinders not returning after two months, would put to sea and make for Port Jackson. To pledge his return, Flinders would leave his precious charts on the sandbank.

The little cutter was renamed *Hope* and, on 26 August 1803, with three cheers from the shore, deeply laden with a company of fourteen men, three weeks' provisions and two small casks of water, it put to sea. Three cheers were answered from the boat, and a seaman on the beach, with permission, ran to the flagstaff, hauled down the upside-down ensign and raised it again with the union uppermost. Flinders later wrote, 'I cannot express the pleasure this little incident gave me'.

And so the great navigator, like Bligh and Edwards before him, set out in a tiny open boat, alone in a vast ocean. Flinders set a course for Sandy Cape at the entrance to Hervey Bay, and on the third day land was sighted. Fifteen days after departing Wreck Reef, the indefatigable Flinders, unshaven but 'not very ragged', walked up the steps to Government House 'to wait upon His Excellency Governor King, whom we found at dinner with his family'.

Plans were quickly put into action to rescue the marooned sailors back on the reef. The merchantman *Rolla*, which was in port provisioning to sail for Canton, agreed to stop at the reef and take any who wished to sail on to that port. The *Francis* would accompany her as far as the reef and bring back those who wished to return to the colony. Flinders would sail in the tiny *Cumberland*, the first ship built at Port Jackson, back to England. Flinders described her as 'a wretchedly small ship in which to traverse fifteen thousand miles of ocean'. After a delay of thirteen days, on 21 September they sailed. On Friday 7 October, just six weeks after Flinders had left the marooned men, the ensign on the flagstaff at Wreck Reef was sighted. Flinders wrote, 'The pleasure of rejoining my companions so amply provided with the means of relieving their distress made this one of the happiest moments of my life'.

In one of the more cowardly acts in the annals of maritime history, the *Bridgewater* under Captain Palmer abandoned the stricken ships on the night of the wrecking and sailed north to New Guinea, on to Batavia and thence to Tellicherry in India. From there he sent a report to the Admiralty that there were no survivors from the incident on Wreck Reef. Palmer subsequently sailed out of harbour and the *Bridgewater* disappeared. Her crew was presumed lost at sea.

Orange omelette with white-chocolate sauce

Omelette
2 eggs, separated
2 tablespoons grated orange zest
1 tablespoon cream
1 tablespoon milk
2 tablespoons sugar
butter

Sauce
100 g (3 ½ oz) white chocolate
¼ cup cream
¼ cup orange juice

Whisk the egg yolks, zest, cream and milk in a bowl.

Beat the egg whites to firm peaks, then beat in the sugar. Fold into the egg yolk mixture.

Preheat the oven to 200°C (400°F). On the stovetop, heat a heavy-based, ovenproof frying pan to very hot and seal the surface with a little butter. Drain off any excess butter and pour the egg mixture into the pan. Transfer to the oven and bake for 8–10 minutes.

For the sauce, heat the white chocolate with ¼ cup of water in a saucepan, stirring until the chocolate melts. Stir in the cream and orange juice until smooth.

Come and get it
Use a spatula to fold the omelette in half. Slide out of the frying pan onto plates. Pour the sauce over the top and serve.

Baked forest fruits with meringue

Fruit

225 g (8 oz) fresh or tinned plums, stoned and quartered

225 g (8 oz) cherries

225 g (8 oz) blueberries

¼ cup sugar

225 g (8 oz) strawberries, halved

225 g (8 oz) raspberries

Meringue

3 egg whites

1 ¼ cup caster (superfine) sugar

1 tablespoon cornflour (cornstarch)

pinch of salt

1 teaspoon white vinegar

Preheat the oven to 180°C (350°F). Combine the plums, whole cherries and blueberries in a baking dish and sprinkle with the sugar. Bake for 15 minutes. Stir in the strawberries and return to the oven for another 15 minutes. Remove from the oven and stir in the raspberries. Leave to cool, then chill in the refrigerator.

Preheat the oven to 160°C (320°F). Beat the egg whites to stiff, dry peaks and gradually add ¾ cup of the caster sugar, beating until dissolved.

Combine the remaining sugar, cornflour and salt. Lightly fold into the egg whites along with the vinegar.

Lightly butter a baking tray and mound the meringue in pretty dollops the size of generous tablespoons over the tray. Bake until the meringues show the first signs of colouring, then turn the oven down to 120°C (250°F). Bake for a total of 45 minutes. The meringues should be only lightly coloured. Leave to cool in the oven.

Come and get it

Spoon the cold baked fruits onto plates and top each with a meringue.

Apple, pear and Californian mission–fig tart

I have a Californian mission-fig tree growing in my garden. They have dark fruit with a distinctive strong flavour. The dried figs are small and can be purchased from specialty shops, or you can use regular dried figs (although they won't have quite the same pungency).

Pastry
125 g (4 oz) butter
60 g (2 oz) icing (confectioners') sugar
1 lemon, zested
1 egg yolk
55 g (2 oz) almond meal
150 g (5 oz) plain (all-purpose) flour, sifted

Filling
2 ripe pears, cored and finely sliced
2 Granny Smith apples, cored and finely sliced
1 cup golden caster sugar
7 star anise
15 dried Californian mission figs, sliced open

Combine the butter, icing sugar and lemon zest in a bowl and beat until creamy. Beat in the egg yolk, then fold in the almond meal and flour. Cover and refrigerate for 20 minutes.

Preheat the oven to 220°C (430°F). Butter a pizza tray. Roll the dough on a floured surface to the diameter of the tray. Place the pastry on the tray and return to the refrigerator for 20 minutes.

Mix apples, pears and caster sugar in a bowl. Heap the apple, pear and sugar mix roughly over the pastry.

Scatter the star anise and mission figs over the top. Bake in the oven for 20 minutes. Pour off any excess juices, sprinkle with the remaining sugar and return to the oven for 15 minutes.

Come and get it
Serve cool or warm, cut into slices.

The Star of Greece

God chooses some of us to do certain work here on earth before we go, possibly to bring happiness to others, and some he takes away at the very threshold of life.

Carl Claeson, survivor of the wreck of the *Star of Greece*

According to the ancient superstition of sailors, Friday the 13th is a day of dread, but no one could have foreseen the catastrophe that was to unfold when, on 10 July 1888, the *Star of Greece* was piloted out of Port Adelaide to an anchorage in the Semaphore Roads.

Built in 1868 in Belfast by Harland and Wolff, the *Star of Greece* was a steel-hulled three-masted ship, 227 feet long and 35 feet wide, and weighed more than 1200 tons. On the morning of Thursday 12 July 1888, Captain Harrower, a 29-year-old Scot, was piped aboard, and appeared 'perfectly sober'. The ship was loaded with 16 000 bags of wheat bound for the United Kingdom and had a ship's company of twenty-eight. The anchor was weighed at 6 p.m., and under a moderate wind the captain set a course south for the Backstairs Passage, the strait between Cape Jervis and Kangaroo Island. At around 10 p.m. the wind shifted to the south-west and blew with great force. Not wanting to negotiate the passage at night in such weather, Harrower had the ship hove to. Why he didn't head for open sea, or towards the Port of Ardrossan, where he could have sheltered in the lee of Yorke Peninsula, is a mystery to this day. The heavily laden vessel was shipping much water over the decks in the wild squalls, and in the darkness had drifted 15 miles off course. At around 2 a.m. Harrower ordered the port anchor to be dropped. Sixty fathoms were let out, but the anchor was fouled and failed to catch ground. The ship drifted helplessly towards the Willunga Reef.

Able Seaman Carl Claeson was at the helm when

all of a sudden a great mountainous breaker came roaring along and lifted the ship up in the air as if it had been a ball and then set her down on a rocky bottom with a terrible crash that shook her from stem to stern, and the wheel went spinning out of my hands round and round impossible to hold.

Huge waves rolled over the vessel as Claeson made his way up the mizzen mast, then down the mizzen rigging to the poopdeck. Beneath him, the wheat was bubbling out of the hatches. The roar of the sea and the pounding of the ship on the rocks was terrific; water swept away the deck houses; and from above spars, yards and tackle were tumbling everywhere. For the rest of the night the men hung on for dear life, mostly up to their waists in water.

At around sunrise, local resident Thomas Martin spotted the wreck just 650 feet off the coast. He immediately saddled his horse and galloped to the Aldinga telegraph station, and wrote a telegram to the secretary of the marine board in Adelaide to send rocket apparatus. Astonishingly, the message was not received until 9.40 a.m., as the telegraph line didn't open until 9 a.m., and finally, at around 10 a.m., the harbour master at Normanville responded that he would dispatch his rockets—the only ones on the coast—by horse and cart. Meanwhile, an awful scene was unfolding on the beach before a crowd of onlookers and would-be rescuers. Bodies of drowned sailors were coming in on the crests of waves.

All of a sudden the rear half of the ship broke away and turned over, taking four crewmen with it. An hour later, the captain, who, one witness later stated, had been standing in the companionway swigging from a bottle of brandy, attempted to swim ashore together with the second mate, but they drowned instantly in the boiling sea. Several futile attempts were made to send a line to shore by tying a rope around a wooden chest and hurling it overboard, but the ebb tide kept taking it back.

Thomas Tuohy, the mounted constable from Willunga, arrived on the beach at around 10 a.m. Seeing one of the crewmen exhausted and being tossed about in the furious sea, he divested himself of his uniform and dived into the waves, which were between 10 and 20 feet high. After fifteen minutes the drowning man was successfully brought to shore. Nearly exhausted, Tuohy returned to the sea to attempt to save another crewmember, but a terrific wave broke over them, and only after a full minute did Tuohy resurface. The crewman never did.

The rocket apparatus finally arrived at dusk, but it was too late. It would take at least an hour to unload it and transport it over the dunes to the beach. In full view of the crowd, the final two crewmembers left on board attempted to swim to safety. The first was a youth, who survived only one wave before disappearing. The second was the old sailmaker Gustav Carlson. He dived into the wild sea and clung desperately to a floating spar, but a giant wave broke over the ship and he too disappeared from view.

Today, Port Willunga is a popular swimming beach, a 45-minute drive south of Adelaide. The bare, grassy hills of the Fleurieu Peninsula drop spectacularly down to the Gulf St Vincent. Every now and then, great black storm clouds gather over the gulf and squalls whip the sea into a frenzy, but mostly a Mediterranean climate prevails, and gentle waves lap the golden, sandy beach where at low tide you can gaze out upon the Willunga Reef and still see the remains of the *Star of Greece*, a solemn memorial to eighteen lost souls and the worst maritime disaster in the history of South Australia.

Mango bavarois with coconut sorbet

Bavarois
4 gelatine sheets
1 cup milk
2 eggs, separated
50 g (2 oz) caster (superfine) sugar
1–2 mangos
½ cup cream

Sorbet
1 gelatine sheet
¾ cup sugar
400 ml (13 fl oz) coconut milk

For the bavarois, soften the gelatine in a bowl of cold water.

Bring the milk to the boil in a heavy-based saucepan then remove from the heat.

Beat the egg yolks and sugar until pale, then gradually pour in the hot milk, beating constantly. Wipe out the saucepan and return the mixture to it. Gently heat, stirring constantly, until the mixture coats the back of the spoon.

Squeeze the excess water from the gelatine and stir into the custard until dissolved. Leave in a cool place until the mixture is almost set.

Remove the flesh from the mangos and purée in a food processor. Measure out 1 cup and fold into the custard along with the cream.

Beat the egg whites to firm peaks and fold them into the mixture. Pour into lightly buttered moulds and refrigerate overnight.

For the sorbet, soften the gelatine in a bowl of cold water.

Put the sugar and 1 ½ cups of water in a saucepan and bring to the boil, stirring until the sugar dissolves. Remove from the heat, squeeze the excess water from the gelatine and stir into the syrup until dissolved. Stir in the coconut milk. Freeze in an ice-cream machine to the manufacturer's instructions. Otherwise, pour into a tray and place in the freezer. When almost frozen, pulse the mixture in a food processor, return to the tray and refreeze.

Come and get it
Briefly dip the bavarois moulds in hot water, then shake onto plates and serve with scoops of sorbet.

A–Z OF AUSTRALIAN SEAFOOD

The number of aquatic species living in Australia's oceans is astonishing. The CSIRO lists over 4400 fish and 14 000 marine invertebrates including molluscs, crustaceans, sponges, stony corals and the like.

The names for fish can be confusing, differing from place to place. For example, mulloway is also known as butterfish, kingfish or jewfish. In order to clear up considerable confusion in the marketplace, various government agencies have joined forces with fish taxonomists, anglers, aquarists and the fishing industry to try and create a uniform list of Australian fish names.

I have not included an exhaustive list of all Australian seafood—a book in itself—but rather a selection of the most common and readily available, listed from A to Z.

Abalone

Abalone have one shell and a large muscular foot that attaches itself by suction to hard surfaces. The most popular types occur in the cooler waters of southern Australia, the four most prized being blacklip, brownlip, Roe's and greenlip, the last the most prized of all. Abalone is harvested wild by licensed divers and is increasingly farmed both locally and offshore. They are very expensive shellfish, so it is great when you come across them snorkelling or diving off a remote beach—take a knife with you to remove them from the rocks. There is generally a bag limit of five per person per day that varies slightly from state to state.

To remove abalone from their shells, place a sharp filleting knife against the inside of the shell and move it inward, cutting the muscle attachment as close as possible to the shell. Carefully remove the meat. The head, gills and viscera can be eaten; it is personal preference whether you cut away or retain them.

As a general rule, cook abalone either fast and furious or slow and gentle. They can be sliced thin and barbecued or even sliced thin and eaten raw as sashimi.

Barracouta

The barracouta is a common catch in Victoria and Tasmania (not to be confused with the barracuda of tropical Australia). They are shiny silver fish with a protruding lower jaw, very sharp teeth and sharp spines in their gills. Barracouta hunt in schools, so when they are on, they are often all you will catch; sometimes they even jump out of the water and latch on to your lure! As kids we would often catch 'couta, but our parents would only bother cooking them if they were all we had. The flesh is a little oily and is at its best smoked.

Barramundi

This magnificent fish is found in tropical Australia and the Indo-Pacific as far north as southern China. In Thailand it is called *pla kapong khao*. Barramundi is farmed all over Australia and elsewhere—even the UK! A curious fish, they are protoandrous hermaphrodites, meaning they start life as males and at around five years of age, change gender becoming prodigious egg producers—one female was recorded with 17 million eggs. They tend to inhabit estuaries, entering coastal waters to spawn. Australian anglers go crazy for these fish: they can be big, they fight, and they taste great, especially the wild ones.

Barramundi has lovely, firm, flaky flesh that is extremely versatile in the kitchen. It can be baked, fried, barbecued, steamed or tossed in a wok. The big fish can be cut into cutlets. Barramundi works well as a substitute for Northern Hemisphere recipes calling for sea bass. Beware of shysters trying to pass frozen, imported Nile perch off as barramundi; it is a similar fish but nowhere near as good.

Blue-eye trevalla

Blue-eye trevalla is caught in cooler waters down the east coast, around Tasmania and off South Australia. It is particularly popular in Tasmania, where you can also buy the smoked roe. Blue-eye trevalla is a firm-fleshed fish with large flakes that holds together well, making it very versatile.

Bake blue-eye trevalla with a breadcrumb, lemon zest and parsley crust. It is also one of the best fish to stir-fry because it holds together so well.

Blue grenadier

Blue grenadier is a deep-water fish with very soft flesh and thin, blue skin. It is ideal for making Thai fish cakes.

Bonito

Australian bonito swims on the east coast from southern Queensland to Wilsons Promontory. They are sometimes called horse mackerel and are found to depths of about 30 metres, growing up to about 1.8 metres in length and weighing up to 9 kilograms, although they are usually caught at around 4 kilograms. They have strong, pink, flaky flesh and should be bled after catching. Bonito is best eaten fresh rather than frozen and goes well with strong flavours.

Bream

Bream are one of the most popular recreational species, but are wily and not always easy to hook. They are related to snapper and live in coastal and estuarine environments, swimming upstream to spawn. The coastal fish are silver, while the estuarine tend to be darker and have a stronger flavour. Yellowfin bream occur all the way down the east coast to Victoria, but black bream are more plentiful in the south, ranging from New South Wales all the way to southern Western Australia. Frying-pan bream inhabits the tropics, caught from Brisbane to Shark Bay.

When cleaning bream, be sure to remove all the white fat from the abdominal wall as it can taint the fish. Bream goes with citrus and any Asian flavours, and because of its shape, works well in a bamboo steamer.

Bugs

The undignified name 'bug' belies the wonderful flavour of these marine crustaceans—the only catch is that all the meat is in the tail, and it seems the bigger they grow, the less meat they have, perhaps meant as a barb for the greedy shopper. Moreton Bay bugs occur from Exmouth in Western Australia around the north coast to Coffs Harbour in New South Wales, although they are named after Brisbane's Moreton Bay. They are a bycatch of the prawn and scallop industry so are more available during the prawn season. Balmain bugs are fairly similar to their Moreton Bay cousins, although a bit fatter and their eyes are in the middle of their heads. They are harvested in waters up to 650 metres deep and occur from Southport in Queensland all the way around southern Australia to Geraldton in Western Australia.

Bugs can be cooked almost any way you can imagine. They are handy boiled and then chilled and added to seafood salads. Try slicing them in half lengthwise through the shell and grilling them over charcoal with a marinade of ginger, garlic, chilli, lime juice and coriander (cilantro).

Clams, cockles and pipis

The bi-valve mollusc is not only good for bait; it is also great to eat! I love Goolwa cockles, which are found just beneath the wet sand at the water line along the beach near the mouth of the Murray River in the Coorong. Just by scooping your hand into the sand you can easily pick up a good feed of cockles. Put them in a bucket of sea water and leave them for up to 24 hours. Kick the bucket every so often—this will cause the cockles to release any sand or grit.

Clams, cockles and pipis can be boiled and soused in vinegar; combined with fish in a chowder; steamed in a bamboo steamer and served with a dip; or cooked in a hot wok with Asian flavours.

Coral trout

These delicious tropical reef fish have a mild, sweet flavour and moist, white flesh with fine flakes. They are versatile and present beautifully with their bright skin on. I like them deep-fried whole, Asian style, and I never forget to eat the cheek meat!

Crabs

The wonderful **blue swimmer crab** inhabits most of Australia's coastline, but is commercially harvested mainly in south-east Queensland, the gulfs of South Australia, south-west Western Australia, Shark Bay and the Pilbara coast. They favour shallow, sandy and estuarine waters, where they move around according to the moon, tide and—if you believe local crabbers—all manner of supernatural forces!

Crabbing is great fun—wandering around the mudflats and mangroves in a pair of shoes (for obvious reasons) with a rake and a bucket. On seeing the telltale claws pointing out of the mud, slide the rake underneath and scoop the crab into a bucket. Sometimes you can get enough crabs for a feed in a couple of minutes; sometimes nothing all day.

The meat of the blue swimmer is moist, sweet and nutty. It's great in pasta, but I love to boil blue swimmers whole in sea water and serve with a sauce such as duck-egg mayonnaise. Once immersed in boiling water, their shells change from blue to bright red.

The **king crab** is the second-largest crab in the world after the giant crab found in waters off Japan. It can weigh over 13 kilograms, has an unusual purple and creamy white shell when raw, and a huge pincer that sometimes has so much meat inside that it makes a great steak! Despite their size, their flavour is sweet and their flesh tender. You will need a seriously large pot to boil these up. They are delicious boiled in sea water. The picked meat is great tossed in a salad with lettuce, avocado and a lime dressing.

In the estuaries of northern Australia, amid the tidal mudflats and mangroves, you can find the wonderful, feisty **mud crab**. Beware their claws—they are strong enough to cause serious injury. They can survive out of water for several days, but freshly caught is best. I love eating Singapore chilli mud crab (page 33) on the Gulf of Carpentaria. The crabs turn blue when boiled, for which it is best to use salt water. But my favourite way to cook them is chopped in large pieces and wok-fried as the shells impart lots of flavour.

Spanner crabs occur all around Australia's north, but are chiefly harvested from Coffs Harbour to Rockhampton on the east coast. Named for their spanner shape, they are a versatile crab with sweet white flesh. I like boiling spanner crabs and reserving the liquid for tom yum (page 16). I scoop out the meat and serve it with avocado, fresh salsa and wild rocket (arugula).

Dory

Legend has it that St Peter brought the John Dory to Christ; the spot on its side is St Peter's thumbprint. It uses its spot to frighten would-be predators. There are other dories too—king dory, silver dory and mirror dory, but John Dory is best. However, the head and abdominal cavity are large, which means there is a small amount of flesh relative to the size of the fish.

Dory has a delicate, distinctly sweet white flesh with very fine flakes. I like to fry fillets in a pan skin-side first and serve with fresh tomato and basil; olives and pancetta; or hot extra-virgin olive oil and balsamic vinegar.

Eel

The eel is an extraordinary creature. It spawns in the Coral Sea, then the larvae float with the current 3000 kilometres down the coast of Australia. They enter rivers and estuaries from Richmond in northern New South Wales to Mount Gambier in South Australia. The larvae that travel upstream are female, while those that remain in estuaries are male. For up to 35 years the eels live in the river before returning to the Coral Sea to spawn and die. The Kerrup Jmara Aboriginal people of Lake Condah in western Victoria built a complex system of stone traps to effectively harvest eels for both consumption and trade.

Smoked eel is great tossed with beetroot, rocket (arugula) and goat's curd with an extra-virgin olive oil and balsamic vinegar dressing and fresh tarragon. Poached eel is popular in Europe; the poaching liquid turns to jelly when cooled. Eel cutlets are great sizzled on a hotplate and served with a spicy tomato sauce.

Emperor

There are several species of emperor that inhabit both the Pacific and Indian oceans in tropical and semi-tropical waters. My favourite is the red emperor. It has delicious moist white flesh.

If cooking whole, it is especially important to remove the gut and gills that can taint the flavour, and be sure to remove the blood vein along the spine.

I like to deep-fry emperor whole, cutting slits in the sides so it cooks evenly, and top it with lemongrass, chilli, garlic, shallots and coriander (cilantro). Emperor is also great baked whole, wrapped in foil and stuffed. Or try marinating filleted emperor in a soy and sake mixture then frying it in a hot pan. When the fish is cooked, remove it and reduce the remaining sauce.

Flathead

If there is one fish I love, it is flathead. Not the prettiest of fish, but underneath is the sweetest, fine-textured white flesh. I have so many memories of fishing for flatties in Port Phillip as a child. Sinker over the side, wait a few seconds for a bite and reel them in! Beware of the sharp spikes behind the head. With correct filleting they are boneless and have become very expensive to buy over the past few years.

My grandmother used to fry them in beer batter and we kids would wolf them down with mayonnaise. Grandma would treat any bone stuck in our throats by making us swallow a wad of white bread. I also like flathead tails with North African sauces.

Flounder

Flounder reminds me of summer holidays. We kids would get a broom handle, fasten a long nail to the end and tie a dolphin torch to the top. We'd then wander about the sandbanks in knee-deep water after dark spearing flounder. It's a wonder we never speared ourselves!

Flounder are flat fish that lie on one side of their bodies with their eyes on the opposite side. There are several species: greenback, spotted, longsnout, smalltooth and largetooth. They are found all around the Australian coastline and inhabit estuaries and shallow bays.

Flounder is delicate fish and is nice simply dusted with flour and pan-fried whole, served with lemon wedges.

Garfish

When the 'gars' are running, you're sure to get a feed. If you fish for them on light tackle they fight like miniature marlin. They are found in estuaries and bays and love seagrass and man-made structures like jetties. On Kangaroo Island I have seen them in the thousands. They are fussy eaters though, and you often need to change your bait. They are also a bit finicky to fillet and bone, although the bones are so fine some people don't bother. Some like to run a beer bottle or rolling pin along their backs to crush the bones before removing the backbone.

Garfish are traditionally dusted with flour and pan- or deep-fried and served with lemon wedges.

Gemfish

Gemfish are a silver fish with a protruding lower jaw. They live on the edge of the continental shelf in temperate waters of southern Australia—from Exmouth, Western Australia, around to Fraser Island, Queensland—and are fished commercially off the south-east coast. They were very popular in restaurants in the 1970s and the fishery was subsequently greatly diminished.

Gemfish have great firm flesh and lend themselves to curries, stir-fries and skewering on kebabs.

Gurnard

If you can be bothered going to the trouble of filleting these bottom-feeders, they are deliciously sweet. Beware the savage spikes that can cause excruciating pain.

In the cooking department, simple is good—dust the fillets in flour, fry in butter and serve with a few slices of fried lemon.

Herring, Australian

The Australian herring closely resembles its cousin the Australian salmon but is much smaller, growing up to around 40 centimetres in length but averaging 15–20 centimetres. These wonderful little fish have always been known as tommy ruffs in South Australia, where they are much loved.

Ranging along the southern coast from Queenscliff in Victoria as far north as Shark Bay in the west, they are caught all year round. Easy to catch from a jetty, they often run at the same time as squid and garfish—at dusk or tide change. Use a float and a light tackle, and remember to burly—they love white bread and once you get onto them, you will be pulling them in like mad!

Herrings are oily fish and I love butterflying them, dusting them in flour and deep-frying until crisp, then serving them with a dipping sauce of fish sauce, lime juice and chilli. They are also great smoked.

Leatherjacket

Much maligned and disliked by anglers because they steal bait, leatherjackets are tasty eating providing you gut them immediately.

Leatherjackets are good on the barbecue. I fillet them leaving the leather on, brushing kecap manis (sweet soy sauce) or extra-virgin olive oil and balsamic vinegar onto the flesh side, then remove the leather after cooking. They are also good in curries.

Ling

Rockling inhabits estuaries and shorelines, while pink ling prefers deeper open water. The flesh of both is excellent, flavoursome and moist.

Ling holds together well, making it good to stir-fry. But my favourite way to cook rockling is cut in large bite-sized chunks and dipped in a batter containing sesame seeds and deep-fried.

Luderick

Only in Victoria are luderick called by their correct name; elsewhere they are known as blackfish or blackies. They are a small, dark fish with a cream belly that occur down the east coast of Australia to western Victoria and the northern coast of Tasmania. Once caught, they should be bled and skinned immediately, for if they have been feeding on weeds they can have an unpleasant flavour.

Large luderick are good baked whole—just make sure you have cleaned any black matter from inside the gut cavity, then stuff it with chopped onion, garlic, cubed pancetta, parsley and Spanish sweet smoked paprika. Rub the outside of the fish with butter, add a glass of pinot noir to the tray, and bake at 180°C (350°F) for 45 minutes.

Mangrove jack

Mangrove jack is a sea perch that inhabits estuaries and reefs in northern Australia. They are lightning-fast, have sharp teeth like a dog and provide great sport-fishing.

Mangrove jacks have a firm texture and a delicate yet distinct flavour, and can be cooked in almost any way. I once ate a memorable numus prepared from raw mangrove jacks while watching the sun set between palm trees across the Timor Sea on Melville Island.

Marlin

Marlin is a large billfish with an elongated silver body, spear-like snout and long rigid dorsal fin. They are prized sport-fish as they put on a great fight, as Hemingway detailed in *The Old Man and the Sea*. Striped marlin off the east coast of Australia have been targeted by Japanese long-line fishing vessels. Marlin meat is firm with a strong flavour and is high in oil, similar to swordfish and tuna.

Some people believe eating marlin is unethical given the dwindling population; in America there is a 'Take Marlin off the Menu' campaign. There are also the usual considerations of mercury content as marlin is at the top end of the food chain.

Morwong

Morwong are open-sea fish. They are very wary, but have a mouth that sucks bait and once hooked, they fight like ten tigers.

Morwong has creamy flesh with its own unique flavour. They are great cooked in a bamboo steamer with soy, ginger, garlic, spring onion (scallion) and sesame oil, but also fry and barbecue well. Use them as you would snapper.

Mullet

There are 16 species of mullet found in Australian waters, eight of which are sold commercially. Most have silver bodies covered with large scales. They don't deserve their ho-hum reputation; in the markets, mullet is a well-kept secret, and this has kept their price down. I particularly like the yellow-eyed mullet that is a common catch in the Coorong, South Australia.

Mullet has a pinkish-grey firm flesh, and is sold either whole or filleted. When you catch a mullet yourself and want to cook it whole, thoroughly clean the stomach cavity as it will taint the flavour. For an even milder flavour, fillet the fish and remove the skin.

Mulloway

Walk into any fish and chip shop in South Australia and ask for butterfish; mulloway is what you get, a wonderful fleshy fish with a few large bones. They are also sometimes called jewfish and kingfish, and are found close to shore and in estuaries. Mulloway are often caught in heavy surf, usually at dusk or at night, and can be up to 30 kilograms. They are best bled immediately.

With large flakes and moist white-to-light-pink flesh, mulloway make great eating. Small mulloway are great baked whole, while larger fish make excellent cutlets. I like to dip mulloway in beer batter and deep-fry it.

Mussels

Blue mussels cling to rocks in the wild in many parts of southern Australia. They are indiscriminate filter feeders, so ensure that any you gather are living in absolutely pristine waters. Whereas commercial dredging once harvested gritty mussels from the bed of the sea, today almost all commercially available mussels are farmed on long lines, resulting in a cleaner product without grit. The males tend to have whiter flesh and the females are more orange. Farmed mussels tend to have a thinner shell than their wild cousins.

The meaty New Zealand green-lipped mussel is imported into Australia and is popular eating. Sadly, this mussel has started to inhabit Australian waters, is displacing native species and is considered feral.

Inspect each mussel before cooking. If the mouth is ajar, give it a sharp tap with a knife. If it snaps shut it is alive—if not, I usually open it and carefully smell it. If it is still clean and fresh, it is likely to be only recently deceased and still edible. However, if you are confronted with a long-dead mussel, ditch it! Clean the shells and remove the byssal threads or beard with a sharp downward tug.

The thing to remember when cooking mussels is not to overcook them, as they tend to go rubbery. There are endless ways to cook them: stir-fried in a wok with Thai flavours; soused in vinegar; or cooked in a sauce of tomatoes, onions, garlic, white wine, chilli and herbs. They can also be tossed into pasta or barbecued.

Nannygai

Nannygai, also known as redfish, is not dissimilar in appearance to a small snapper. They occupy waters from Cape York down the east coast and across to the south-west of South Australia. They like to swim next to reefs that drop away to deep water where there is a current. They have a sweet, succulent flesh with a delicate flavour that comes easily off the bone.

Cook nannygai in the same way you would red emperor or snapper: barbecue it, bake it, deep-fry it or try it steamed in a bamboo steamer with lime juice, garlic, fish sauce and kaffir lime leaves.

Octopus

Octopus, with squid and cuttlefish, is a member of the cephalopod family. There are five species of octopus caught commercially in Australia, with the southern octopus a major catch. Baby octopus is farmed locally and imported.

Octopus is a major predator of rock lobsters and often come up in lobster pots to the chagrin of fishers. The lobster industries' disdain for them is typified in such annual events as the annual octopus throw in Port MacDonnell, South Australia. Despite this treatment, lobster fishers are recognising that octopus is in demand and profitable.

Some octopus can be tough. One way to tenderise it is to marinate it in papaya or kiwifruit pulp for a few hours. Octopus is great cooked in olive oil with kalamata olives, garlic and sprigs of rosemary—drop it into enough hot oil to cover it, then turn the heat off and leave the octopus in the oil for 45 minutes, then drain and chop it up. Octopus is also great on the barbecue.

Orange roughy

Orange roughy is a very slow-growing, long-living fish found in deep, cold waters. It is known to be a dwindling species due to overfishing and has been added to Australia's endangered list. Alternative names for it are sea perch, deep-sea perch and red roughy. It belongs to the unfortunately named slimehead family and is not the most attractive of finfish. It needs to be deep-skinned to remove the subcutaneous fat; consumption of this fat can cause diarrhoea. The flesh has a high oil content.

I prefer not to eat orange roughy, but if you must it can be baked, grilled, fried, poached or smoked.

Oreo

Poor oreo would perhaps win the award for the ugliest fish in the market—bulging eyes, a flat body and a very small tail, somewhat typical of fish found in very deep water. But what it lacks in looks it makes up for in flavour: lovely fine-flaked sweet flesh and good rounded fillets with large, easily removed bones. Only the skin is tough and inedible.

Oreo can be cooked the same way as red emperor. Try it steamed in a bamboo steamer with garlic, shallots, fish sauce, lemon juice and lemon slices.

Oysters

The flavour of fresh oysters is the essence of the sea. They are the scent beneath the jetty, the wind blowing off the Southern Ocean, the smell of the rock pool at low tide. In Australia there are several species, including the highly prized pearl oyster, which is the second-highest-earning commercial harvest next to rock lobsters. All commercially available oysters in Australia are farmed; there is no commercial harvesting of wild oysters, but it is a delight for the recreational gourmet to wander around the inlets of southern Australia taking oysters off the rocks and shucking them in situ.

Pacific oysters are the most widely cultivated shellfish on the planet. Endemic to Japan, they are fast-growing and produce a large, plump, flavoursome oyster. The main areas for farming Pacifics in Australia are Tasmania and the Eyre Peninsula in South Australia.

Sydney rock oysters are smaller than their Japanese cousins and occur naturally in the estuaries of eastern Australia. They are slower growing and have a thicker shell. Aficionados claim they have a preferable flavour to Pacific oysters, with a silky, luxurious texture and subtle iodine and zinc flavours. In the wild, they have trouble competing with the introduced Pacifics, which tend to smother them.

Native flat oysters are often called the southern belon because of their similarity to the prized French belon. They have been eaten for thousands of years by Aboriginal people, as evidenced by countless shell middens around the coast. European settlers loved them too and as a consequence, they were nearly harvested out of existence. They require high salinity and grow in estuaries throughout southern Australia. Their meaty flesh has full-bodied flavour.

I like oysters best au naturel: freshly shucked, in their liquor, with a slice of lemon—or in a bloody Mary! If you must cook oysters, they can be lightly poached or baked, and they go well with ginger, garlic, shallots, soy and vinegar. They are also great deep-fried and sprinkled with a spicy salt made with Sichuan pepper.

Perch, Ocean

This pinkish-red fish of southern Australia can be found in shallow water and up to depths of 800 metres. It has delicate moist flesh. When cleaning, watch out for its fin spines.

Ocean perch is great steamed Asian-style, or shallow-fried with a spicy crumb. The bones are full of flavour and are great for stock.

Perch, Sea

There are several species of sea perch in Australian waters including hussar, Moses and saddletail. They have delicate and flavoursome white flesh.

Smaller perch lend themselves to baking, but this perch is versatile and goes well on the barbecue, fried or poached.

Pomfret

Pomfret is found worldwide; in Australia it is fished commercially in southern waters. A finned flat fish, it is caught in open water. Pomfret goes well with Asian flavours and can be baked, barbecued, fried, poached or steamed.

Prawns

Banana prawns are caught by trawlers in northern Australia, the largest fishery being the Gulf of Carpentaria where they are caught in April and May. They range from Shark Bay in Western Australia right across the Top End and down to northern New South Wales. There are two species distinguished by leg colour—red or cream. They are highly fertile little critters—a female can lay up to 400 000 eggs! Recreational fishers net them in estuaries, while commercial operations often net them in the open sea where the prawns come together in great aggregations (where the water 'boils'). I find that banana prawns are best eaten hot rather than cold. They have a mild flavour and hold their shape well.

Bay prawns are small and very sweet, sometimes called river prawns because they can often be found over 30 kilometres upstream from the coast. They are found on the east coast from Fraser Island to Eden. Keen bay-prawners are often seen in the estuaries of New South Wales after dark with nets and torches. They are a great prawn to boil and add to salads.

Endeavour prawns have a distinctive and strong flavour; some would say they are the truffle of the prawn world! They are medium in size and light in colour, ranging from Exmouth in Western Australia across the Top End to the south coast of New South Wales, but are only commercially harvested in the tropics. I like to use them for prawn patties, and they are particularly good in a sweet potato, macadamia and prawn fritter served with a dipping sauce of fish sauce, rice vinegar and coriander (cilantro) root.

King prawns are the show ponies of the prawn world—big, glossy and flavoursome; no wonder they are so popular. They have tan shells with a distinctive blue tail and are found all around the Australian coast with the exception of waters from Cape Otway to Kangaroo Island. King prawns are harvested commercially off the east coast. They work well with a tempura batter or crumbed with Japanese (panko) breadcrumbs. They are excellent grilled on the barbecue and served with a fiery Thai relish.

The **school prawn** found along the east coast is simply called the school prawn; on the west coast it is called the western school prawn. They have white shells and a distinctive taste: very sweet. They are usually purchased cooked because of their short shelf life. If you buy them this way, just a simple dressing or vinaigrette will suffice; they don't need any strong embellishment to cloud their subtle flavour. When dining on the Mekong River in northern Thailand once, I ordered a dish called Dancing Prawns. When it arrived, the bowl had a lid on, and the reason soon became obvious—beneath it was a miasma of tiny, live, freshwater prawns dancing in a dressing of fish sauce, chilli, lime juice and coriander (cilantro). It worked there and it certainly works with school prawns too (although you would have to catch mini prawns yourself).

At the risk of stating the obvious, **tiger prawns** are striated; the three most popular in Australia are black, brown and grooved. Black tiger prawns are farmed along the east coast in tropical and subtropical waters. Tiger prawns look great on the plate. I like to use tiger prawns when making garlic prawns with cream, garlic, parsley and white wine. I use a really hot pan and sear them for just a few seconds, leaving them rare. If you are brave, eat the prawn together with its tail shell and legs: tasty!

Queenfish

Queenfish are caught in Australia's northern waters, sometimes off the continental shelf, sometimes quite close to shore. They are fierce fighters when hooked. The markings down the side of these fish are considered by some Chinese people to be 'God's fingerprints'; in parts of China they are revered as holy. The flesh is firm and dry. Once they have been caught, it is best to bleed them straightaway.

Queenfish make great numus and are also good on skewers because of their firmness. If you plan to barbecue them, marinate them well to prevent them drying out.

Rock cod

There are several species of rock cod found all the way along the east coast, across the north coast and down the west coast. They inhabit estuaries and open water, preferring reef areas. Those caught in open water have a cleaner taste, and the smaller ones make the best eating. Rock-cod flesh has wonderful large flakes and a mild, sweet flavour. They are low in oil and very juicy—the heads are great for stock.

Rock cod is perfect raw in a Tahitian salad (page 102) or numus. It also works well in Thai fish cakes or grilled with chopped salad onion and tapenade.

Rock lobster

There are four varieties of rock lobster, Australia's largest seafood export: southern, eastern, western and tropical, the latter considered superior for sashimi. Commercially and recreationally caught in pots, the flesh is firm, rich and sweet. The tail meat makes up to 42 per cent of the total weight of the lobster, but don't forget the legs and antennae, the sweetest parts.

Boil lobster in stock, or split the tails in half and barbecue, bake, pan-fry or steam them. Serve it hot or cold; toss it in salad; serve it in a curry.

Salmon, Atlantic

Atlantic salmon was introduced into the Derwent River in Tasmania in the 1800s, but after release it disappeared. Another attempt was made in the 1960s, introducing salmon into the lakes of the Snowy Mountains Hydro-Electric Scheme, creating a hatchery that now produces eggs for other operators. Today Tasmania has built successful sea-farming operations and their salmon is widely considered some of the world's best. There is also a small sea-farming operation at Cape Jaffa in South Australia, utilising cold-water upwellings, and some river-farming operations in north-east Victoria. Atlantic salmon has pink flesh with a wonderfully distinctive flavour and is high in Omega 3.

Salmon is best seared on a very hot grill and served rare. It is also delicious smoked; holds together well when baked; and can be fried, steamed or poached.

Salmon roe is available in jars and I like to serve it with sea vegetables, sushi and oysters. Not only does it present well but it is a taste sensation, the al-dente resistance as your teeth break the skin, followed by an explosion of salty delight.

Salmon, Australian

When I was a boy, these were known as bay trout; I guess salmon sounds more upmarket, except they are actually perch and have white flesh. Whatever—they put up a great fight when hooked, usually with a surf rig off the beach during a rising tide. In January, great schools of salmon gather along the New South Wales and Victorian coastlines before migrating to Western Australia, where they are not unknown at 9 kilograms in weight. They spawn out at sea and then move along the bays and estuaries feeding on bait fish. When you land one, slit its head open, remove the gills with a knife and break the backbone by giving it a good whack and pulling the head upwards from the body, then put it upside-down in the sand or in a bucket to bleed. Otherwise, the flesh can discolour and develop an unpleasant taste. Some people remove the strip of red flesh across the middle of the fillet directly under the skin to reduce the flavour, but this should not be necessary if you have bled the fish.

Australian salmon with its strong flavour lends itself to smoking or cooking with a strong sauce. Once on a boat off Wilsons Promontory, I made sashimi out of absolutely fresh salmon and it was memorable eating.

Salmon, Threadfin

Threadfin salmon is found mainly in the inshore tropical waters of northern Australia. You know when you get one on the line; because of their large mouth, they are difficult to hook, but once you have them they put up a spectacular fight. It is a delicious eating fish with firm white flesh, large flakes and a subtle sweet flavour.

Crumb threadfin salmon with breadcrumbs, lemon zest, grated parmesan and parsley and fry in extra-virgin olive oil. The firm flesh also holds together well on the barbecue or as kebabs.

Sardine, Australian

The Australian sardine inhabits southern waters from southern Queensland all the way around to Shark Bay in Western Australia. They are blue on their tops and sides with silver bellies, and were once predominantly used for bait (they are also known as bluebait or pilchards and are excellent for catching Australian salmon, snapper and tailor).

Sardines are great barbecued with spices and they also go well grilled, pan-fried and baked. Try them fried and then marinated in a vinaigrette and served cold. There are endless Mediterranean recipes for them.

Scallops

As a child I used to watch from the beach as the 'scallopies' would trawl up and down the southern end of Port Phillip. It turned out to be a shameful practice that depleted the fishery and destroyed the habitat, which is now only just starting to show signs of an eventual recovery. There are three types of scallops in Australia—the commercial scallop, which is served with the red roe or coral on; the saucer scallop from tropical waters, which has the roe removed; and the amazing queen or Coffin Bay scallop from South Australia's Eyre Peninsula, which has a beautiful purple roe and shell. Don't choose scallops with white flesh as they have been soaking in water, known as 'plumping' in the trade. It increases their weight and size but renders them quite horrible.

Scallops are very easy to cook. There is only one rule: be gentle; scallops are delicate. Overcooked scallops will shrink. Scallops are cooked the moment they turn opaque. They are delicious under a grill with lime juice, extra-virgin olive oil and cracked pepper. They are also great deep-fried or tossed in an Italian tomato sauce. They go well with saffron. Scallops are very versatile; go by the rules but use your imagination.

Sea urchins

It was with great trepidation that I first took a Melbourne fishmonger's advice and drove my knife into these spiny black balls to remove the deliciously rich, sweet orange roe inside. Since my initiation, I have never looked back. I use a tea towel to protect my hand, or you can use gloves.

You don't have to cook sea urchins. The roe is delicious with crusty bread and extra-virgin olive oil, as it is eaten in Catalonia (washed down with an Ampurdán rosé). It mixes well with butter and lemon zest to dress grilled scallops, and Italians toss it into pasta with garlic, hot capsicum or chilli and extra-virgin olive oil. The Japanese flavour custards with it and serve it with sushi.

Shark

Several species of this perfect predator are commercially harvested in Australian waters. In the south, one of the most overfished is gummy shark, sold in fish and chip shops since the 1920s as flake. School shark, angel shark, black tips, whiskery and others are also caught commercially. Generally, the smaller the shark the sweeter the flesh, and the less likely to contain the unpleasant ammonia flavour often found in larger sharks. While sharks are great game fish, always treat them with respect. A landed shark can lie motionless for hours and then unexpectedly lash out and bite the unwary.

Shark has firm and boneless white flesh. It is great for kebabs and stir-fries and battered for fish and chips of course. Always remove the skin before cooking as it will shrink and tear the flesh.

Snapper

Snapper was named by Captain James Cook. The entire lower third of Australia contains snapper grounds. They are a schooling fish that travel in large groups of similar size and age, so when your boat comes across a school, it's on for young and old. They are tremendous fighters; a 10-kilogram snapper will take the best part of 20 minutes to reel in. They have white-to-pink flesh with medium flakes. The larger the fish, the larger the flakes.

I love smaller snapper steamed whole Cantonese-style (page 55). The larger fish are best cut into cutlets and are tasty grilled with extra-virgin olive oil and lemon juice.

Snapper, Tropical

Tropical snapper is a loose term to describe a number of fish including gold-band snapper, green jobfish, king snapper and ruby snapper. These fish should not be confused with southern snapper, although they have the same moist, firm, creamy pink flesh.

Tropical snapper lends itself to Asian flavours. They are versatile and can be baked, fried, barbecued or poached, and are good for sushi and sashimi.

Spanish mackerel

Spanish mackerel has silver skin with hardly any scales. They are a wonderful fish found in waters across northern Australia; I have caught them in the shallows of the Gulf of Carpentaria and served them the following day beneath the rainforest canopy at Lawn Hill Gorge. They travel well—just ensure they are chilled the moment they are caught.

Mackerel can provide a wonderful large cutlet, which I like to poach in champagne with garlic and kaffir lime leaves. Because of their oily texture and great flavour, they are perhaps the supreme barbecue fish, great with Asian dips on the side. It is recommended not to eat mackerel raw, as it has been known to be heavily infested with parasitic worms that can cause illness in humans.

Squid

Squid was once only used for bait, but we know better now! Found all around Australia, these weird-looking cephalopods are great fun to catch—they are very fast in the water and can be caught in the shallows and from jetties. Make sure you wear your old clothes; chances are you'll get covered in ink.

Squid doesn't require much cooking—briefly toss it in a wok or grill it on a barbecue over intense heat. Alternatively, you can opt for a slow braise. Anything in between and you will end up with a tough and rubbery mess. Squid can be crumbed, battered or dusted in spiced flour and deep-fried. You can also stuff the tubes, securing them with a toothpick and baking them. The ink can be used in sauces and as a colouring for pasta and noodles.

Stingray

Captain Cook first called Botany Bay Stingray Bay after the large numbers of rays that the crew of the *Endeavour* caught there. Stingray meat is called skate. There are dozens of species around

Australia with differing quality meat. It has a unique stringy texture with a slightly gelatinous quality and is very versatile.

You can grill stingray, perhaps dusting it with seasoned flour. Stingray is tasty braised: bring it to the boil with stock, onions, celery, garlic and lemon juice, then let it cool in the stock for 20 minutes. You will know it is done when the meat falls from the cartilage easily.

Sweep

Sweep is an attractive silver fish found all around the coastline of southern Australia. The juveniles seem to like New South Wales, whereas larger fish are found from Mallacoota in Victoria right around to Perth. They are a school fish and like estuaries, rocky ledges and areas close to shore. Their firm flesh is ideal for numus and ceviche.

Swordfish

Swordfish could well be described as the steak of the sea. It has a dense meat with a high oil content ranging from white to almost red when uncooked (turning white when cooked), making it ideal for cooking with strong flavours.

Sear swordfish steaks in a very hot pan, then add some fish stock and herbs, turn the steak and continue cooking for about 30 seconds. Serve seared-side up with the juices. Swordfish is also ideal on a charcoal grill.

Tailor

Tailor is a popular fish found in southern Australian waters. It is a good fighter with very sharp teeth. Predatory, it roams in schools and can be caught from a boat—either stationary near a school or trolling—or from the beach. It is best to bleed tailor immediately, thoroughly clean the gut cavity and put it on ice. It has a high oil content and very soft flesh, so it requires careful handling.

Tailor is good smoked, barbecued, baked or fried. Fry some garlic, add tomatoes, dried oregano and black olives and reduce to a thick sauce, then cook tailor fillets in this sauce.

Trevally

There are several trevally caught in Australian waters: big-eye, black, blue-spotted, and silver to name a few. They have a strong flavour and their flesh is dry. Their bones are large and easily removed. Don't freeze trevally as the flesh becomes mushy when thawed.

Thick trevally skin should be removed before cooking, although if steaming it can be easily removed afterwards. I often steam a whole black trevally with deep incisions all the way to the backbone on both sides—the fish presents well but this also ensures it cooks through and is easy to serve as cutlets. Trevally fries well and also makes good sashimi.

Trumpeter

The two most common trumpeters are the striped and bastard. Trumpeters like reefs and are found close to shore and to depths of 300 metres in the cold waters of southern Australia. Due to overfishing, it is not seen inshore as much as it once was. It is a delicious eating fish.

With its firm flavoursome flesh, trumpeter bakes well and is also good barbecued and pan-fried.

Tuna

There are several species of tuna in Australian waters including yellowfin, bluefin and albacore, which has paler flesh. Tuna are beautiful-looking fish, fight aggressively when hooked, and have wonderful firm, succulent flesh. They are perfect for sashimi and sushi. Tuna steaks are best seared on a hot grill and served rare.

Warehou

Blue, silver and white warehous are found in southern waters from the Head of Bight to Eden in southern New South Wales, and in Tasmanian waters. They have dry flesh with a thick fillet and not many bones. As the darker flesh next to the skin has a stronger flavour, it is best to fillet warehou and cut off the skin together with this layer of darker flesh. They marinate well and are delicious grilled.

West Australian dhufish and pearl perch

West Australian dhufish and its east-coast cousin, pearl perch, have lovely thick white flesh that is highly sought after and expensive. Both are blunt-headed fish with protruding lower jaws and spinal fins. They have easy-to-remove bones and suit most styles of cooking, but are particularly good fried in batter.

Whiting

This great fish is caught in southern waters, with the King George whiting the largest and most renowned. Whiting have soft, sweet and delicate flesh that requires careful handling. I like to simply pan-fry freshly caught whiting.

Yellowtail kingfish

A great fighting fish, often found in ocean waters with strong currents like the rough-up in Port Phillip Heads. A medium oily flesh with a medium to strong flavour, kingfish cutlets are great grilled with citrus flavours. I also like to serve kingfish with hollandaise sauce.

A–Z OF SEA VEGETABLES

Agar

Agar is a gelatine substitute derived from sea vegetables. It is white and semi-translucent. You can buy it in bars, threads or powder. It dissolves easily at 85°C (185°F) and sets at room temperature, making it ideal for jellies with fresh fruit. It is used extensively through Asia but was also used in Australia by early settlers.

Arame

Arame is a species of kelp. When bought dry, it resembles black steel wool and can be blanched in boiling water and then refreshed in cold water. It can then be dressed as a salad or used as a topping for oysters, scallops or mussels. Its very delicate seaweed flavour is enhanced with lime juice and fish sauce.

Dulse

Dulse is a broad, flat-leafed red sea vegetable that grows on northern Atlantic and Pacific coastlines. In Iceland it is eaten tossed with butter; in Ireland you can buy it in pubs dried like potato crisps. It is imported into Australia and is great finely chopped in salads or soaked and added to bean dishes.

Hijiki

Dried hijiki is black and needs to be soaked in water for a couple of hours to soften it. It has a strong flavour. Fry some onions and garlic, mix with some cooked pumpkin, hijiki and soy sauce, and wrap in filo—yum! Some government food agencies advise against eating hijiki because of high levels of inorganic arsenic; I suggest moderation is the key.

Kombu

Kombu is a kelp and one of the foods that provides the so-called 'fifth flavour', umami. It is great added to soups and is a key ingredient in Japanese dashi stock. I always add a strip of kombu when cooking beans and pulses—it improves their flavour and aids digestion.

Nori

Similar to the laver that grows around the British Isles, nori is processed into green sheets like paper and is used to wrap sushi. It is also great cut in strips and added to soups, or used to wrap fish before steaming. Nori no tsukudani is a delicious paste made from nori and soy available from Asian shops. Try it on a cracker!

Samphire

This succulent bush with fleshy nodes is found in salty marshes worldwide. In Australia it grows along the coast as well as inland in the desert, although is not nearly as popular here as it is in the United Kingdom or in France where it is known as *passe-pierre*. To cook with samphire, you generally need to gather it yourself. It can be quite salty raw, but blanching reduces this. Samphire can be tossed in a salad or soused in vinegar. The sprigs are great used as a garnish.

Sea cabbage

Also called sea lettuce, sea cabbage is a small, bright-green seaweed that is plentiful around Australia's southern coast. Simply cut it from rocks or jetties, blanch it quickly in boiling water and refresh it. If you overcook it, it can develop a bitter taste. I think of sea cabbage as the salad green of sea vegetables.

Wakame

This green kelp has been eaten in Asia for centuries and is now harvested in Tasmania. It is thought to have arrived attached on Japanese ships. Tasmanian wakame is highly sought after because of the quality of water it grows in. It is sold dried. Reconstituted, it is slippery with a subtle, sweet flavour. I use it in cucumber salads and soups, and love it with fresh oysters and squid-ink pasta.

GLOSSARY

Black moss
Black moss is a vegetable resembling dark, extremely fine vermicelli or hair (it is sometimes called hair moss or hair seaweed). It is a freshwater alga that grows in the Gobi Desert. When soaked in water it takes on a soft texture. It goes by the Chinese name *fat choy* and is readily available in Asian supermarkets.

Chinese brown bean paste
A dark paste of fermented soy beans, water and salt, usually thickened with flour and containing garlic and a little chilli. It is often used to flavour stir-fries.

Chinese rice wine
Often known as yellow wine or Shaoxing wine, this is made from fermented glutinous rice. I use the Pagoda blue label, which is available from Asian supermarkets. You can use dry sherry as a substitute.

Japanese (panko) breadcrumbs
These breadcrumbs are particularly light and fluffy and are available from Asian supermarkets.

Kecap manis (sweet soy sauce)
Kecap manis is an Indonesian soy sauce with a thick syrupy texture due to a high palm-sugar content. I use the ABC brand.

Kudzu
Sometimes known as kuzu, this is the dried root of a legume. Used by Chinese physicians to treat alcoholism, the complex starch molecules make an ideal thickener. Use as you would cornflour.

Maltose
Maltose imparts quite a different flavour of sweetness to regular sugar, more akin to palm sugar. Like a thick treacle, maltose is easily obtainable from Asian and health-food stores.

Matzah
Matzah are Jewish unleavened flatbreads that are sold as dried crackers and are also ground into matzah meal, which is used as flour in dishes such a gefilte fish.

Mirin
This Japanese sweet rice wine has a culinary use similar to sherry. It can be used as a dip with soy sauce for sushi, or even to remove the taste of slightly old fish. Do not use it heavily as it has a strong flavour.

Palm sugar
This brown sugar made from palm sap has a more subtle sweetness than cane sugar. It is sold in cakes and cylinders in varying shades.

Shrimp paste
Paste made from fermented shrimp. *Blachan* is the Indonesian variety that comes in blocks, while *gapi* is the Thai variety that is softer and comes in tubs; it is used across South-East Asia. Don't be put off by the pungent odour; it is an essential ingredient in Asian cooking.

Sichuan pepper
The tiny pod of an Asian fruit, not related to pepper at all. Sichuan pepper has a sweet, aromatic flavour and a tingling effect on the tongue.

Thai chilli paste
Called *nam prik pao*, this is a medium–hot dark chilli paste from Thailand with garlic, shallots, dried shrimp and other ingredients. The jar I buy is the Pantainorasingh brand labelled 'Thai chilli paste with soya bean oil' and has a yellow lid.

Yellow rock sugar
This Chinese sugar comes in yellow cubes and imparts a rich, honey-like flavour.

SOURCES

Mutiny and Massacre: The *Batavia* and Her Miscreant Supercargo

Dash, M, *Batavia's Graveyard: The True Story of the Mad Heretic Who Led History's Bloodiest Mutiny*, Weidenfeld & Nicolson, 2002.
Drake-Brockman, H, *Voyage to Disaster*, University of Western Australia, 1995.
Edwards, H, *Islands of Angry Ghosts*, Hodder & Stoughton, 1966.
Pelsaert, F, *The Voyage of the Batavia*, Hordern House, 1994.

Bungaree: Australia's First Aboriginal Circumnavigator

The Australian Antique Collector, periodical, n.d.
Flinders, M, *A Biographical Tribute to the Memory of Trim*, Angus & Robertson, 1997.
Flinders, M, *Terra Australis: Matthew Flinders' Great Adventures in the Circumnavigation of Australia*, ed. and introduced by T Flannery, Text Publishing, 2000.
Hadlow, J, 'Volunteer Exhibition Guiding Notes', National Library of Australia, 1998.
Haig, C & W Goldstein (eds), *The Aborigines of New South Wales*, National Parks & Wildlife Service, 1980.
Horden, M, *King of the Australian Coast*, Melbourne University Press, 1997.
National Treasures from Australia's Great Libraries, exhibition catalogue, National Library of Australia, 2005.

Seven Weeks in a Leaky Boat: The Journey of the *Bounty* Launch

Australian Dictionary of Biography, vols 1 & 2, Melbourne University Press, 1966.
Bligh, W, *A Voyage to the South Sea*, George Nicol, 1792.
——*A Narrative of the Mutiny, on Board His Majesty's Ship* Bounty; *and the Subsequent Voyage of Part of the Crew, in the Ship's Boat*, George Nicol, 1790.
Dening, G, *Mr Bligh's Bad Language: Passion, Power and Theatre on the* Bounty, Cambridge University Press, 1992.
National Treasures from Australia's Great Libraries.

The *Géographe* and the *Naturaliste*

Bonnemains, J, E Forthsyth & B Smith (eds), *Baudin in Australian Waters: The Art Work of the French Voyage of Discovery to the Southern Lands, 1800–04*, Oxford University Press, 1988.
Clark, CMH, *A History of Australia*, vol. 1, *From the Earliest Times to the Age of Macquarie*, Melbourne University Press, 1962.
Hunt, S & P Carter, *Terre Napoleon: Australia through French Eyes, 1800–1804*, exhibition catalogue, Historic Houses Trust of New South Wales, 1999.

The Theft of the *Ferret*

Evans, WP, *Through the Rip*, Rigby, 1978.
'A Steamer Stolen: How a Glasgow Firm Was Swindled', *New York Times*, 25 June 1881.
Vallance, HA, *The History of the Highland Railway*, Stockwell, 1938.
Williamstown Chronicle, 30 April 1881.

Firestorm at Cape Naturaliste

Lighthouses of Australia, 2002–06, www.lighthouse.net.au/lights/WA/Cape%20Naturaliste/Cape%20Naturaliste.htm#History, viewed June 2009.

Commander, Governor, Pirate, Admiral

A Charge of Mutiny: The Court-Martial of Lieutenant Colonel George Johnston for Deposing Governor William Bligh in the Rebellion of 26 January 1808, National Library of Australia, 1988.
Australian Dictionary of Biography: Online Edition, Australian National University, 2006.
Clark, *A History of Australia*.
Hughes, R, *The Fatal Shore*, Vintage, 2003.

The Loss of the *Cataraqui*

The Annual Register 1846, Longman, Rees, Orme and Co., 1847.
British Parliamentary Papers 1846
Lemon, A & M Morgan, *Poor Souls They Perished: The* Cataraqui, *Australia's Worst Shipwreck*, Hargreen, 1986.
Park, M, *Thrilling Stories of the Ocean*, Henderson, 1852.
TheShipsList, 1997–2009, www.theshipslist.com

Ian Fairweather: 'I've Gone with the Wind'

Australian Dictionary of Biography.
Hetherington, J, *Australian Painters: Forty Profiles*, Cheshire, 1963.
McCulloch, A, *The Encyclopedia of Australian Art*, 3rd edn, revised & updated by S McCulloch, Allen & Unwin, 1994.

The *Loch Ard*

Charlwood, DE, *Wrecks and Reputations*, Burgewood Books, 1996.
Loney, J, *The Loch Ard Disaster*, J Loney, 1970.
——*Victorian Shipwrecks*, J Loney, 1971.

Betsey Broughton and the Burning of the *Boyd*

Australian Dictionary of Biography.
Broughton, W, letter to D Gasperde de Rico, 1814, NLA Manuscript Collection, MS 9707.
Burke, D & A Ferguson, *The World of Betsey Throsby: Discovering Australia's Colonial Past in the Southern Highlands of New South Wales*, Kerever Park, 1994.
McLauchlan, G, *Great Tales from New Zealand History*, Penguin, 2005.
McNab, R, *From Tasman to Marsden: A History of Northern New Zealand from 1642 to 1818*, Wilkie & Co., 1914.
Read, Richard, 1814, *Portrait of Elizabeth Isabella Broughton, about Seven Years Old, 1814*, watercolour, 36.3 x 30.3 cm, National Library of Australia, http://nla.gov.au/nla.pic-an4862493
Roxburgh, R, *Throsby Park: An Account of the Throsby Family in Australia 1802–1940*, NSW National Parks and Wildlife Service, 1989.
Whangaroa, comp. EV Sale, Whangaroa Book Committee, 1986.

The Adventures of the *Tom Thumb*

Currey, CH, 'Bryant, Mary (1765–1794+)', *Australian Dictionary of Biography*, vol. 1, Melbourne University Press, 1966.
Estensen, M, *The Life of Matthew Flinders*, Allen & Unwin, 2002.
Flinders, M, *A Voyage to Terra Australis*, G & W Nicol, 1814.
Hughes, TS, *Matthew Flinders*, Movement Publications, 1991.
Pottle, FA, *Boswell and the Girl from Botany Bay*, Heinemann, 1938.
Smith, S, *Sailing with Flinders: The Journal of Seaman Samuel Smith*, Corkwood Press, 2002.

Lost at Sea: The Sydney to Hobart Yacht Race 1998

Topp, D, 'The Sydney—Hobart Yacht Race 1998: A Legal Perspective', *Australian and New Zealand Maritime Law Journal*.
Stone, R, personal papers and correspondence.

Matthew Flinders: Shipwrecked!

Estensen, *The Life of Matthew Flinders*.
Flinders, *A Voyage to Terra Australis*.
Hughes, *Matthew Flinders*.
Smith, *Sailing with Flinders*.

ACKNOWLEDGEMENTS

First, a huge thank you to my publisher Tracy O'Shaughnessy for her sage advice throughout the project and for always having a steady hand on the tiller. To my researcher Jenny Hadlow, whose years of volunteer work at the National Library of Australia and a love for all things maritime proved indispensable when tracking down obscure minutiae from our nation's remarkable maritime history. My thanks and appreciation to Gayle Goldsmith for sharing her kitchen and her culinary talent generously, assisting me with the desserts, both in their creation and during the photo sessions. As I rarely eat them they remain my greatest challenge in the kitchen. To the team on Phillip Island: Noel and Jenny Murray for domiciling the image crew in their place at Cowes, Bob and Pat Baird for their knowledge and driftwood collecting, and John Jansson for sharing with us his father's remarkable collection of maritime artefacts. My thanks to Dimitrios Goulas from Conway Fish Trading Co. in Footscray for providing fabulous seafood, for which they are renowned. To the student gardeners at Collingwood College for their wonderful warrigal greens, and while I would normally pick them on the banks of an outback creek, they manage to grow them in an inner Melbourne suburb. To the late Jim Black, from whose library I unearthed a small sample of the inspiration that I found in him. To Wendy Jubb-Stoney, for sharing with me and cooking her wonderful curried mutton-bird recipe. A special thanks to my brothers-in-law Cha Rodden, who worked tirelessly during the photo shoot and let me use his magnificent recipe for pipis, and Fergus McErlean, fisherman extraordinaire—no fish in South Australian waters can feel safe in his presence. His revision of the dictionary of seafood was much appreciated. Thanks to Liz Waldron for the loan of her books and helicopter pilot Ray Stone for sharing his inspiring story of bravery and selflessness while saving the lives of many yachties caught in the horrendous storm during the 1998 Sydney to Hobart Yacht Race. To my mother and father for allowing me to spend so much of my childhood on boats and, like so many millions of Australians, develop a deep and passionate love for the sea in all her moods. Finally, a special thanks to my wife and partner in life Jane, who always charts a smooth course, keeps the wind in my sails and manages to see the positive in every situation. Without her endless patience I could never enjoy the indulgence that is writing books.

PICTURE CREDITS

INDEX

guacamole, 186
gurnard, 240

H
harissa, 186
herring, Australian, 240
hijiki, 247
hollandaise, 193
hot and sour prawn soup, 16

I
Indonesian snapper, 80

J
jellyfish salad with chicken and daikon, 174
jewfish *see* mulloway

K
kao niow dahm, 220
king crabs, 239
King George whiting with lemon, capers and parsley, 72
kingfish *see* mulloway; yellowtail kingfish

L
leatherjacket, 241
lime sauces, 71, 137, 144
ling, 241
lobster, 244
    in bisque, 10
    butters for, 190–1
    buying, xii, xiii
    sautéed tails with whisky and lime, 28
    storing, xiv
luderick, 241

M
mackerel, 245
maître d'hôtel butter, 187
mango bavarois with coconut sorbet, 236
mangrove jack, 241
marinated oyster and smoked salmon salad over bitter greens, 138
marlin, 241
mayonnaise, 191
meringue with baked forest fruits, 230
Mesopotamian carp, 78
midye dolmasi, 150
Moreton Bay bugs, 239
    in bisque, 10
morwong, 241
moules à la marinière, 134
mud crabs, xii, 22, 33, 239
mullet, 241
mulloway, 241
    tempura, with black-bean sauce, 116
mussels, 241–2
    à la marinière, 134
    with balsamic vinegar, 126
    with basil and Thai chilli paste, 131
    in bouillabaisse, 4
    buying, xi
    cooked in the sand, 137
    in squid-ink linguine with seafood, 180
    storing, xiv

    stuffed, 150
    with tomato, preserved lemon and saffron, 140
mutton-bird curry, 177–8

N
nam pa prik, 185
nam prik narok, 185
nannygai, 242
    steamed with lime, 88
New England clam chowder, 6–7
nigiri, 107
nori, 46, 107, 119, 247
North African bonito with tomato, chickpeas and preserved lemon, 101
nuoc cham dipping sauce, 36

O
ocean perch, 243
octopus, 242
    with Costa Rican rice, 162
    Galician-style, 167
orange, almond and date salad, 200
orange omelette with white-chocolate sauce, 228
orange roughy, 242
oreo, 242
oysters, 128, 242–3
    buying, xi
    marinated with smoked salmon, with bitter greens, 138
    storing, xiv

P
pannacotta
    green tea and white chocolate, 215
    pandan, 222
pearl perch, 246
perch, 241, 242, 243, 246
    in Tanzanian masala, 86
pipis, 239
    buying, xi
    in chowder, 6
    storing, xiv
piri piri, 24, 40
poaching fish, xvi, 3, 46, 58, 86, 112
pomfret, 243
    baked coconut masala, 94
prawns, 243
    banana, with spicy salt and piri piri, 24
    bisque, 10
    in bouillabaisse, 4
    butters, 190–1
    buying, xii, xiii
    crumbed, with salsa verde, 34
    grilled, with piri piri, 40
    in rice-paper rolls with pork, 36
    sauces for, 185, 186
    in squid-ink linguine with seafood, 180
    and sweet potato ukoy with sawsawan vinegar sauce, 42
    tiger, barbecued, with basil nam prik, 30
    in *tom yum goong*, 16
pulpo á feira, 167

Q
queenfish, 243–4

THE MIEGUNYAH PRESS

This book was designed and typeset by Phil Campbell.
The text was set in 9.5 point The Serif Semi Light with 14 points of leading (text) and
10.25 point Avenir Book with 14 points of leading, 9.75 point Avenir Book with 14 points of leading
and 10.5 point Janson Text with 14 points of leading (recipes).
The text is printed on 128 gsm matt art paper.

THE
MIEGUNYAH
PRESS